The Book on Entrepreneurship and Property

The Guide to Successful Entrepreneurship and Property Investment

Selchouk Sami

authorHOUSE®

AuthorHouse™
1663 Liberty Drive
Bloomington, IN 47403
www.authorhouse.com
Phone: 1-800-839-8640

Published by AuthorHouse 4/2/2013

ISBN: 978-1-4817-8618-8 (sc)
ISBN: 978-1-4817-8619-5 (e)

Table of Contents

Foreword

Are you a budding entrepreneur, business person or someone looking to learn and be inspired by entrepreneurship? For the budding entrepreneur the world of business may appear alluring and exciting. However, business owners do experience great difficulty whilst aspiring to achieving success, and for the spectator entrepreneurship can be a very interesting topic to learn about as you'll find out if you read this book! As a recognised businessman and mentor I advocate that start ups and existing business owners are open to seeking help and guidance to ensure the route to success is short and as problem free as possible. I look to the best and learn from them!

Selchouk is a well respected practising property solicitor with entrepreneurial flair. He has applied his passion in writing this very interesting and compelling book that illustrates how entrepreneurship has developed over the years and what we can expect from the future with the Third Industrial Revolution. He draws lessons from 10 entrepreneurs that he regards most highly in history, and elaborates on his recent piece in the Business Reporter for The Daily Telegraph entitled "Essential Factors for Business Success". The property entrepreneur also greatly benefits from a guide on legal issues that one should consider when purchasing a property which also includes how it is possible to acquire a property for as little as £1.

This book will excite you about entrepreneurship and guide you towards the path of success. Selchouk's legal background ensures that the book is not overly complex but rather fluent and easy to absorb with each page packed full of golden nuggets.

Raymond Aaron
NY Times Best-Selling Author

Introduction

This book illustrates how entrepreneurship has developed and impacted society over the years by reviewing the industrial revolutions that have set the framework for modern economic development. It then moves on to the list of the ten greatest entrepreneurs of all time. The book also illustrates the importance of collaboration and creative partnerships and how the entrepreneurial mind set can be applied to property investing to be able to acquire a property for as little as £1. There is nothing better than learning from the best to awaken the entrepreneurial spirit. The final chapter contains useful information that can be referred to during the book. By the time you have completed this book, you should be equipped with the fundamentals to enable you to decide what your next move in business is going to be; whether it is to find the right business partner or to seek advice from an expert.

Opportunities are always around, even during periods of recession as we are experiencing today. The great entrepreneurs know how to grab or create opportunities and then make it happen by forming the right partnerships. Chapter 7 elaborates on the finding by the Global

Entrepreneurship Monitor (GEM) that entrepreneurship globally is on the rise and that entrepreneurship, is the best hope for stimulating a weakened world economy.

Chapter 1

The Three Industrial Revolutions

The Industrial Revolution 1760-1850

Entrepreneurship and innovation fuelled the Industrial Revolution. This was a period in history that transformed human life by changing the way people made a living and the products available to them resulting from the rise in manufacturing. This revolution was an economic one in England, spreading throughout Western Europe, North America, and Japan, and eventually, the rest of the world. England had capital, a large population and people with scientific knowledge and entrepreneurial skills, which were the social and economic factors that helped make the Industrial Revolution possible. As businesses took off, increases in demand by the working class, because of population growth and advertising, further fuelled the revolution.

The most important innovations during this period advanced the production of textiles. Steam power produced from coal was used in the iron industry and transport with the steam-powered locomotive, and within the new factories that began to open up, together allowed the economic take off, which defined the Industrial Revolution.

The revolution began in Derby in England. Because of the inventions during this time, and improvements made to them, English weavers were working around 200 times more cotton in 1850 than they did at the start of the revolution.

The improved steam engine invented by James Watt was at first mainly used to power pumps for pumping water out of mines, but from the 1780s it was applied to power other types of machines. Rapid development of efficient semi-automated factories grew in places where waterpower was not available. For the first time, people did not have to rely on animal, human, water or wind for power. The steam engine was used to lift coal to the surface of mines; pump water from coalmines; to blow air into the furnaces for the making of iron; to grind clay for pottery; and to power new factories of all kinds. The Industrial Revolution began to rely on coal to produce the high temperatures needed to smelt iron. Over time, it also became a source of heat for the steam engine. In the Iron industry, coke eventually replaced charcoal to improve the process of iron smelting. For over a hundred years, the steam engine played a key role in the progress of industry enabling purchasing power in Great Britain to double and the total national income to increase by a factor of ten.

One of the major developments of the Industrial Revolution was the large factory. Businessmen began employing families in the countryside to spin and weave. This was known as the domestic system, where all members of the family participated in the production. The business owner provided the materials and was responsible for the marketing. Over time, the factory system developed in the late eighteenth century with the invention of machines. The factory was more cost effective as it allowed the concentration of machines and workers in one place reducing transportation costs and allowing for greater quality control. The factory owner had greater control of the workers and could enforce much stricter discipline. The factory floor applied what the economist Adam Smith termed "division of labour," whereby each worker became an expert in one area of production, thereby increasing his efficiency. Workers did not have to switch tasks during the day, which further saved time and money, thereby enabling Victorian factories to grow throughout the nineteenth century.

As industry expanded, so did the transportation network for raw materials and finished products with the development of thousands of miles of canals and all-weather roads. The main innovation in transportation of the nineteenth century was the railroad. The railroads were driven by steam-powered, coal burning locomotives that provided quick, reasonably priced transportation, to areas that could not be reached by water. The construction of railroads created a demand for iron and for large numbers of workers and became a large industry in its own right.

The population of England doubled between 1680 and 1820. This increase provided the large supply of cheap labour needed by the factories. It also led to an increase in demand for manufactured goods. British agriculture also experienced significant change. The process of enclosure allowed landlords and farmers to fence in their fields and control production. Then by introducing crop rotations land owners greatly increased their yield. They also introduced scientific breeding to improve the quality of their herds. This resulted in an increase in productivity with a reduced number of agricultural workers. This permitted more people to leave the farms to work in the factories while supplying them with cheap food.

During this period, England pioneered the scientific revolution, and therefore had plenty of people with the scientific knowledge to startup businesses. It also had a merchant capitalist class who organized the domestic system. The combination of these two ingredients is aptly illustrated by the partnership of Matthew Boulton and James Watt. Watt had the scientific knowledge and Boulton was a leading entrepreneur who was able to assemble the workers with the needed skills to mass produce Watt's engine, which arguably is the most instrumental innovation that defined the Industrial Revolution.

The Industrial Revolution spread to the rest of Europe and North America over the course of several decades after it developed in Britain. The successes of the technological changes were so profound internationally that for over a century, Great Britain became the leading industrial nation.

Second Industrial Revolution 1890-1940

In the late nineteenth century, new technologies changed the face of manufacturing in Europe, which led to new levels of economic growth that were accompanied by a strong desire for business expansion. Electrical communication converged with the oil-powered internal combustion engine, resulting in the Second Industrial Revolution. The electrification of factories gave rise to the era of mass-produced manufactured products, the most significant being Mr H Ford's automobile. Henry Ford mass-produced his gasoline-powered Model T car. Virtually overnight, millions of people began to trade in their horses and buggies for cars. To meet the increased demand for fuel, the new oil industry started exploration and drilling. The United States became the leading oil producer in the world. Within two decades, vast cement highways were laid out across America, and American families began moving to new suburban communities that only a few years earlier were isolated rural hamlets. Thousands of miles of telephone lines were installed. Later, radio and television were introduced; recasting social life and creating a communication grid to manage and market the far-flung activities of the oil economy and auto age.

For the public, the revolution was marked by mass production of consumer goods and the mechanization of manufacturing to serve the needs of an increasing population. Technological leadership shifted from the United Kingdom to the United States and Germany.

The First Industrial Revolution was driven by coal, steam, and iron. The Second Industrial Revolution came about because of innovation in steel, electricity, and chemical technologies. Steel was harder, stronger, and more malleable than iron. Between the 1850s and 1870s, three different processes for defining and mass-producing alloy steel were developed. In turn, steel production soared with shipbuilders changing to steel construction. By the end of the century, large power stations were able to send electric current over great distances. In 1879, Thomas Edison invented the incandescent-filament lamp and turned electricity into light. The demand for electricity soared; very soon, whole towns were electrified. The chemical industry was the third important new technology that contributed to this industrial revolution. The efficient production of alkali and sulphuric acid transformed the manufacture of consumer goods such as soaps, paper, fertilizer and textiles.

Besides the sudden development in industries, many other changes were taking place. Department stores were developed and were a symbol of urbanization. In addition advertising began to develop which was apparent from the colourful and bold posters of the late nineteenth century advertised, bicycles, and sewing machines, concert halls and soaps.

As capitalist institutions began to rise, a great amount of capital was needed to fund large-scale businesses, so entrepreneurs needed to offer better guarantees on investors' money. To facilitate this, most European countries improved limited-liability laws, which said that shareholders could lose only the value of their shares in the event of insolvency. Generally, there was significant shift toward larger businesses because of a desire for increased profits. Towards the end of the 19th century, most European nations had legislated for the principle of limited liability. Large sums of personal capital became available, and the transferability of shares allowed a degree of business continuity not possible in other forms of enterprise.

The Third Industrial Revolution

The great economic revolutions in history occur when new communication technologies converge with new energy systems. For example, with the Second Revolution electrical communication converged with the oil-powered internal combustion engine. Today, Internet technology and renewable energies are beginning to merge to create a new infrastructure for a Third Industrial Revolution (TIR), as identified by Jeremy Rifkin, that will change the way power is distributed in the 21st century.

It is envisaged that in the future, hundreds of millions of people will produce their own renewable energy in their homes, offices, and factories and will share green electricity with each other in an "Energy Internet", just as information is now generated and shared online. The creation of a renewable energy regime, loaded by buildings, partially stored in the form of hydrogen, distributed via a green electricity Internet, and connected to plug-in, zero-emission transport, paves the way for a Third Industrial Revolution.

In the past making things involved taking the constituent parts and screwing or welding them together. Now a products can be designed on a computer and manufactured "printed" on a 3D printer, which produces a solid object by creating successive layers of material. The digital design can be altered with a few mouse clicks. The 3D printer can run unmanned, and can make many things which are too complicated for a traditional factory to produce. In time, these extraordinary machines may be able to make almost anything, anywhere from your home to a remote village. This is known as additive manufacturing.

Already, hearing aids and high-tech parts of military jets are being printed in bespoke shapes. The geography of supply chains will change. An engineer working in a very rural area of the world, who finds he lacks a certain tool, no longer will have to have it delivered from the nearest city. He can just download the design and print it. The days when projects grind to a halt because of missing parts, or when customers complain that they can no longer find spare parts for equipment or goods they have purchased, may indeed eventually be a thing of the past!

New materials are lighter, stronger and more durable than the old ones. Carbon fiber is replacing steel and aluminum in products ranging from mountain bikes to airplanes. New techniques let engineers shape objects at a tiny scale. Nanotechnology is giving products enhanced features, for example bandages that help heal cuts, engines that run more efficiently and plates that cleans more easily. With the Internet allowing ever more designers to collaborate on new products, the barriers to entry are falling. At the time when Ford needed vast sums of money to open his factory, his modern equivalent can start with as little as a laptop and a desire to invent.

In the same way that the Internet radically reduced entry costs in generating and disseminating information, giving rise to new businesses like Google and social media platforms like Facebook and Twitter, additive manufacturing has the potential to greatly reduce the cost of producing hard goods. This makes entry costs sufficiently lower to encourage hundreds of thousands of mini manufacturers -- small and medium size enterprises (SMEs) to challenge and potentially out compete the giant manufacturing companies that were at the centre of the First and Second Industrial Revolution economies.

The reduction in transaction costs are leading to the accessibility of information, energy, manufacturing, marketing, and logistics. This new era of distributed capitalism is likely to change the very way we think of commercial life in the 21st Century.

On May 29th, 2012, the European Commission held a conference in Brussels with the theme, "Mission Growth: Europe At The Lead Of The New Industrial Revolution." Manuel Barroso, the President of the European Commission, and Antonio Tajani, Vice President and Minister of Industry and Entrepreneurship, co-hosted the summit. Vice President Tajani called for a comprehensive Third Industrial Revolution economic agenda to regrow the European economy and create an integrated European single market. In his speech, Vice President Tajani said:

"Today is a good day for all of us, because today is the beginning of the Third Industrial Revolution. Now the European conversation will go beyond austerity, straight to creating growth and jobs in Europe. My slogan is: 'Without a new industrial policy, no growth, no jobs...'"

"...the first industrial revolution was the revolution of coal and steam, the second was the oil one. This Third Industrial Revolution is the Internet of energy and is not only about energy. It involves many key sectors, from raw materials, to manufacturing, services, construction, transport, Information Technologies and even chemistry."

"...because its energy sources are distributed and not centralized, and therefore scale laterally and not centrally,

[The Third Industrial Revolution] is the ideal playground for SMEs.... our 2020 strategy puts us on the right path but we must now accelerate and put more resources on growth, and this must be based on sustainability, testing the edge of our technological frontiers..."

Jeremy Rifkin followed Vice President Tajani's address with a keynote speech on the Third Industrial Revolution vision and game plan for realising the European dream.

For a thought provoking summary of Jeremy Rifkin's keynote speech "Beyond Austerity" in which he advocates implementing the "Road Map" for a Third Industrial Revolution visit www.entrepreneurshipandproperty.com

Chapter 2

10 of the Greatest Entrepreneurs of All Time

The entrepreneurs listed below can be described as pioneers, inventors, or magicians who have created products and services that have had significant positive social and economic impact. Many have not only promoted positive entrepreneurship on a global scale, but also have applied their entrepreneurial skills for the benefit of charitable causes.

Especially prepared for this book visit www. entrepreneurshipandproperty.com to receive a top 10 from John Warrillow Founder and President of the Sellability Score

1 James Watt & Matthew Boulton

As identified in Chapter one the Industrial Revolution took off with the arrival of steam power. It began to replace waterpower and muscle power (which often came from horses) as the main source of energy in use in the workplace. Its first use was to pump water from mines. The early steam engines were not very efficient, but a double-acting rotating version created by Scottish mechanical engineer and inventor James Watt gave engines the power to become a driving force behind the Industrial Revolution. Steam power was used not only in engines, but also in locomotives, furnaces and other factory equipment that were difficult to use before to the invention of steam power.

The steam engine evolved from the atmospheric engine invented by Thomas Newcomen in 1712 and began to be used in different industries, not just in mining, where the first engines had been used to pump water from underground. Early mills had run successfully with waterpower, but by installing a steam engine a factory could be located anywhere, not just near to water.

In 1775, Watt formed an engine-building and engineering partnership with businessman Matthew Boulton. The partnership of Boulton & Watt became one of the most important businesses of the Industrial Revolution and served as a creative technical centre for the most part of the British economy. The partners solved technical problems and spread the solutions to other companies. The technological advances of the Industrial Revolution developed more quickly because firms began to share information, which they then could use to create new techniques or products.

From mines to mills, steam engines found many uses in a variety of other industries. The advent of steam engines improved productivity and technology, and gave rise to the creation of smaller and more efficient engines.

After Richard Trevithick's development of the high-pressure engine, different modes of transport became possible, and steam engines powered boats, railways, farms and road vehicles. Steam engines are an example of how industrialization resulted in changes, which in turn led to even more changes in other areas.

Matthew Boulton also aspired to produce the best coins. He succeeded, and the firm of Boulton and Watt went on to make not only coins, medals and tokens, but also the steam engines that drove England to lead the industrial revolution.

2 Thomas Alva Edison.

This is the man who gave the world the electric light, talking motion pictures, the phonograph and over 1,000 other patented inventions. Whilst he was arguably one of the world's greatest inventors, he also was able to exploit the profit potential in his creations. His impact on the way people live was and is pervasive. The combination of inventive genius and entrepreneurial flair made him great.

Thomas Alva Edison was born to Sam and Nancy Edison on February 11, 1847, in Milan, Ohio, America. Edison was the youngest of his six other siblings. From an early age, he showed a fascination for mechanical things and for chemical experiments.

In 1859, Edison took a job selling newspapers and sweets on the Grand Trunk Railroad to Detroit. In the baggage car, he set up a lab for his chemistry experiments and a printing press where he started the *Grand Trunk Herald*, which was the first newspaper to be published on a train. An accidental fire is said to have forced him to stop his experiments on the train.

Around the age of twelve, Edison lost almost all his hearing. There are different theories as to what led to the loss of his hearing. Some believe it was the after effects of scarlet fever, which he had as a child. Whilst others point the finger to a conductor boxing his ears after Edison caused a fire in the baggage car, an incident that Edison claimed did not take place. He blamed it on an incident in which he was grabbed by his ears and lifted to a train. His loss of hearing did not discourage him, instead he we was even more determined by seeing it as a positive as it meant that he could shut out noises and disruptions around him and focus on researching material and carrying out experiments.

In 1862, Edison rescued a baby from a track where a boxcar was about to roll into him. Mr J.U. MacKenzie, who was the child's father in return, taught Edison railroad telegraphy as a thank you. Later on in the same year, he took a job as a telegraph operator in Port Huron, Ohio. At the same time, he continued his scientific experiments on the side.

In 1868, Edison moved to Boston where he worked in the Western Union office and worked even harder on his inventions. In January 1869, Edison resigned from his job, with the intention of devoting himself to the creative pursuit of inventions. The electric vote recorder, in June 1869 was his first invention to receive a patent. Acknowledging that politicians were reluctant to use the tool, he decided that in the future he would not waste valuable time and energy inventing equipment that no one wanted to use.

During the next period of Edison's life, he participated in projects and partnerships dealing with the telegraph. In 1877, Edison worked on a telephone transmitter that greatly improved on Alexander Graham Bell's work with the telephone. His transmitter made it possible for voice transmission to be made at higher volume and with greater clarity over standard telephone lines. Edison experimented with the telephone and the telegraph that led to the invention of the phonograph in 1877. He realised that sound could be recorded as indentations on a rapidly moving piece of paper. He eventually created an invention with a tinfoil coated cylinder and diaphragm with a needle. When Edison spoke the words "Mary had a little lamb" into the mouthpiece, it played the phrase back to him. The Edison Speaking Phonograph Company was formed in 1878 to market his creation. Unfortunately, eventually the initial novelty factor of the phonograph wore off, and Edison turned his attention to what would be his most highly recognized invention of all.

He began to focus on the electric light system, setting aside the phonograph for almost a decade. With the support of financiers, The Edison Electric Light Co. was founded in 1878 to carry out experiments with electric lights and to own any patents resulting from them. In return for assigning his patents to the company, Edison received shares in the business. Their aim was to build the incandescent bulb and an entire electrical lighting system that could support a city. A filament of carbonized thread proved to be the key to a long-lasting light bulb. Lamps were installed in the laboratory, and many people journeyed out to Menlo Park to view and understand the new finding. A special public exhibition at the laboratory was held for the masses on New Year's Eve.

Edison was determined to prove the commercial viability of electric lighting. In 1881, he set up an electric light factory in East Newark, New Jersey and in 1882 installed the world's first commercial lighting system in the financial district of Lower Manhattan, New York. In 1911, Edison's companies were restructured into Thomas A. Edison, Inc. As the company grew and diversified the founder became less involved in the day-to-day operations by delegating, although he still had some decision-making authority. The company began to focus more on maintaining market presence than to produce new inventions frequently.

Henry Ford who you will be reading about next in this book was a friend of this great inventor who reconstructed Edison's invention factory as a museum at Greenfield Village, Michigan, in 1929.

3 Henry Ford.

The second industrial revolution began in America in the early 20th century with the assembly line, which "drove" the era of mass production with Henry Ford pioneering the way. Ford fundamentally changed human lifestyles by making available a vehicle, the Model T, that greatly extended people's range of movement. The car allowed Americans to populate every corner of the country. However, his more profound impact targeted industry. The moving assembly line that he designed to build his cars was the preeminent breakthrough of the Industrial Age. Ford earned the seed capital for his enterprise by working as an engineer at the Edison Illuminating

Company in Detroit. Henry Ford was born on July 30, 1863 being the eldest of William and Mary Ford's six children. He grew up on the family farm in what is today Dearborn, Michigan and enjoyed a childhood typical of the rural nineteenth century, which included spending days in a one-room school and doing farm chores. Just as you would expect from very successful figures in history his interest started from an early age. It was an interest in mechanical things which enthused him, and which distracted him from his farm chores.

In 1879, sixteen-year-old Ford left home for the nearby city of Detroit to work as an apprentice machinist for three years and then returned to Dearborn. During the next few years, Henry split his focus between operating and repairing steam engines, finding temporary work in a Detroit factory, and over-hauling his father's farm equipment, including lending a reluctant hand with other farm work.

After two failed attempts to establish a company to manufacture cars, the Ford Motor Company eventually incorporated in 1903 with Henry Ford as vice-president and chief engineer. The company manufactured only a few cars a day at the Ford factory on Mack Avenue in Detroit. Teams of two or three worked on each car from components made to order from other companies.

In 1908, Henry Ford realized his dream of manufacturing an automobile that was reasonably priced, reliable, and efficient by introduction of the Model T. The car started a new era in personal transportation. It was easy to drive, maintain, and handle on rough roads, which quickly become a great success.

By 1918, half of all cars in America were Model

Ts. The company opened a large factory at Highland Park, Michigan, in 1910 to meet the increase in public demand. Here in 1913, Henry Ford combined precision manufacturing, interchangeable and standardized parts, and a division of labour, with a continuous moving assembly line. Workers occupied a station in the factory, adding one component to each automobile as it moved past them on the assembly line. Delivery of parts by conveyor belt to the workers was timed carefully to ensure that the assembly line moved fault free and efficiently. The advent of the moving assembly line revolutionized automobile production by greatly reducing assembly time per vehicle, which lowered costs. Ford's production of Model Ts made the company the largest car manufacturer in the world.

Between the period 1910 and 1920 the company began construction of the world's largest industrial complex along the banks of the Rouge River in Dearborn, Michigan. The plant included all the elements needed for car production: a steel mill, glass factory, and assembly line. Iron ore and coal were transported in to the plant on steamers and by railroad, which was used to produce both steel and iron. Rolling mills, forges, and assembly shops transformed the steel into axles, springs and car bodies. Foundries converted iron into engine blocks and cylinder heads that were assembled with other parts into engines. Towards the end of 1927, all steps in the manufacturing process from refining raw materials to final assembly of the automobile took place at the Rouge Plant, perfectly demonstrating Henry Ford's idea of mass production.

Ford has become one of the world's largest and most profitable companies, which is also one to survive the great depression, which started in the US in 1930.

4 Ray Kroc

Ray Kroc was 52 when he discovered a small restaurant run by the McDonald brothers through his business as a kitchen equipment salesperson. He liked the idea of a restaurant with a limited menu and wanted to make the McDonald's restaurant a name all over the world. Perseverance was instilled in Kroc throughout the years before he founded McDonald's and during the time it took to build up the empire, he never stopped working. Success can come at all stages of life.

Kroc laid the foundation for the modern fast-food industry and created the world's No. 1 fast-food chain. Kroc began working early in life. While still in grammar school he started a lemonade stand in front of his home in Chicago and he also had a job in a grocery store, and he spent a Summer working the soda fountain in his uncle's grocery store. From these early experiences, Kroc began to see the world as one large marketplace.

By the time he was a teenager, Kroc had no interest in school, so he left to take a job as a salesperson for Lily-Tulip Cup Co. He was a talented. Young, ambitious and hard working, Kroc quickly became the company's top salesperson. During this post selling cups, Kroc met Earl Prince; a client who had invented the Multimixer which was a five-spindle milk shake-mixing machine.

Fascinated by the speed and efficiency of the machine and recognizing its potential, Kroc, then 37, left Lily and purchased exclusive marketing rights to the machine. He spent the next decade and a half travelling the country peddling the Multimixer to numerous diners and restaurants.

As Kroc approached his 50th birthday sales began

to drop. During the early 1950s people started to leave the cities for the suburbs, forcing many soda fountains to close. This caused Ray to start losing customers very quickly. Just as he thought his luck was on the out one small restaurant in San Bernardino, California, ordered eight machines. Curious to find out who placed the order, Kroc left for California to see what kind of restaurant needed to churn out 40 milk shakes at a time. Upon arrival, he found it to be a small hamburger stand run by Dick and Mac McDonald who were brothers.

The McDonald brothers' restaurant was different to other restaurants. By comparison to the popular drive-in restaurants during that time, it was self-service, had no indoor seating, and the menu included only hamburgers, cheeseburgers, fries, drinks including milk shakes; all of which were produced in an assembly-line style that enabled customers to place their orders and receive their meals in less than a minute.

Kroc quickly calculated the financial rewards possible with hundreds of these restaurants across the country. However, when he approached the McDonald brothers with the idea, they told him they were not keen on taking this task themselves. This gave Kroc the opportunity to offer to do it for them. The two brothers agreed, and gave Kroc the sole rights to sell the McDonald's method.

He opened his first McDonald's in April 1955 in Des Plaines a suburb of Chicago. He used the spotless and efficient restaurant as a showroom for selling McDonald's franchises to the rest of the country. For each franchise sold, Ray collected 1.9 percent of the gross sales. From that, he would give the two brothers one-half percent. In the first year Kroc sold 18 franchises but was shocked to discover he was barely making enough money to cover his expenses. As he rushed to purchase the rights to the McDonalds' methods, he had made them a deal they could not refuse. Unfortunately, it was a deal on which he could not make any money.

Kroc then met Harry Sonneborn, a financial genius who showed Kroc how to make money, not by selling burgers, but by selling real estate. Under Sonneborn's guidance, Kroc set up a company that would acquire or lease the land on which all McDonald's restaurants were situated. Franchisees paid Kroc a fixed monthly rental for the land or a percentage of their turnover, whichever was greater. By owning the land that the franchises were built on, Kroc was guaranteed a profit. With his real-estate magic formula in place, Kroc set out to achieve his target of having 1,000 McDonald restaurants from coast to coast.

He then acquired all the rights to the name from the McDonald brothers; by 1965, he succeeded in opening more than 700 restaurants in 44 states. In April of the same year, McDonald's became the first fast-food company to go public making Kroc an instant multimillionaire. By the end of the decade, Kroc had reached and exceeded his target, with nearly 1,500 McDonald's operating worldwide.

By the 1970s, McDonald's was the largest food supplier in the US and would remain so through the next two decades. On January 14, 1984, which is the day he died, a new McDonald's was opening on average every 17 hours!

Like many of the 20th century's most influential entrepreneurs, Ray Kroc was not a creative. When Kroc came onto the scene, convenience food existed in many forms, from local diners to hot dog stands. However, Kroc had the ability to understand all the complexities of the fast-food game and deliver it in the best possible way.

Ray Kroc believed that the success of his company lay in his franchisees following everything that constituted "the McDonald's Method". To ensure that this was achieved, he developed a 75-page manual that set out every aspect of running a McDonald's chain. The instructions were clear which left nothing to interpretation. The burgers had to be exactly 1.6 ounces, served with a quarter ounce of onion, a teaspoon of mustard with a tablespoon of ketchup. The manual also specified how often the restaurant needed to be cleaned.

In 1961, Kroc came up with a way to gain even greater control over his franchisees. He opened a training centre that would eventually become Hamburger University, where students earned their degrees in "Hamburgerology" with a minor in French fries. It opened in the basement of a McDonald's in Elk Grove, Illinois.

The golden arches is now a super brand with over 25,000 McDonald's in operation globally today. In 2012, McDonalds sponsored the Olympics, which was largest global event in the world. The brand continues to evolve to ensure it stay fresh and strong in the market place.

5 Steve Jobs

For the full text and video clip of Steve Jobs' Stanford Commencement Speech visit www.entrepreneurshipandproperty. com.

Steve Jobs and business partner Steve Wozniak weren't the first Silicon Valley entrepreneurs to launch a billion-dollar business from a Palo Alto garage-Hewlett and Packard were there before them-but they were the first to create a machine whose use was so wonderfully intuitive that even technophobes embraced it to create the most valuable company in history.

Apple's surging stock has pushed the company's value to up to around $624 billion, the world's highest, ever. With a market value of about $460 billion Apple is worth more than Google, Golman Sachs, General Motors, Ford, Starbucks and Boeing put together. Apple Inc. has been the world's most valuable company since the end of last year. It is now worth around 54 percent more than No. 2 Exxon Mobil Corp. Apple will begin to fall if it stops producing such innovative products as it has in the past, although it is showing few signs of slowing down.

The late Steve Jobs built this empire based on the concept that everyone should own a computer, and that computers should be user friendly. He was one of the first to advocate this view. The computers that he built for the masses were smaller compared to mainframe systems, greatly cheaper, user-focused and accessible.

Born in 1955, and given the name Steven Paul Jobs, he grew up in Silicon Valley, the California location where technology thrived. As a child, Jobs learned about electronics with his father, usually in the family's garage where he would take things apart and rebuild them. When he reached high school, he spent considerable time at the head office of Hewlett-Packard, where he met his future business partner, a computer engineer and creative genius named Steve Wozniak. Wozniak, who was shy and reserved, gave Jobs the independence in executing the selling and marketing strategies which made the partnership so powerful and creative - leading to Jobs arguably becoming the greatest marketer and CEO in the world.

In Jobs' biography (*'Steve Jobs' by Walter Isacsson*), recalling his first interaction with Wozniak While sitting on the sidewalk in front of Bill Fernandez's home (*Woz's Homestead High School friend*), Jobs concluded: "Woz was the first person I'd met who knew more electronics than I did. Woz was very very bright."

Wozniak's father (*Francis*) was a rocket scientist at Lockheed Martin, who qualified at the California Institute of Technology. Since he was a child, Wozniak would spend hours gazing at circuit diagrams and take pleasure hearing about the power of transistors and diodes from his father. In the fourth grade, he made an intercom system, connecting his friends' bedrooms in six households. He started making calculators when he was in the eighth-grade. By the time he moved to the penultimate year of high school, he had started playing pranks with his creations. Such was his madness, that when it came to experimenting with new electronic equipment he was even sent to a juvenile detention centre for scaring his school principal with a fake electronic bomb. Although his creations were not commercially viable, they were definitely signs of a genius inventor in the making.

Jobs completed high school and enrolled in college, but that was only for a short period, as he left a few months later. For a short period he worked at video game giant Atari, but then decided to travel to India on a spiritual journey. Returning home, in 1976, Jobs and Wozniak created Apple Computer, working out of the Jobs' family garage. The two entrepreneurs wasted no time, quickly creating a personal computer that sold for about six-hundred-and-seventy dollars. The Apple I turned over three-quarters of a million dollars in sales. Incredibly, when the Apple II was released, sales increased exponentially, beyond all expectation, to one-hundred-and-thirty-nine million dollars.

In 1980, just four short years after forming the company, Apple Computer, Inc, went public, being the largest IPO since Ford Motor Company went public in 1956. The company had a market valuation of US$1.778 billion at the close of day one.

Around 1983, Steve Jobs lured John Sculley away from Pepsico Inc. to serve as Apple's CEO and a couple of years later the two clashed, leading to Jobs' resignation. Wozniak also resigned from Apple.

During this period, Jobs founded Next Inc. a new computer business making high-end innovations for universities. He also bought Pixar from "Star Wars" creator George Lucas for $10 million.

In July1993, the company reported a quarterly loss of $188 million. CEO Sculley was replaced by Apple president Michael Spindler, Apple was restructured and Sculley resigned as chairman.

A couple of years later, Pixar's "Toy Story," the first commercial computer-animated feature, became a huge success and Pixar advanced to Wall Street with an IPO that raised $140 million.

In 1996, Apple announced plans to buy Next for $430 million in order to obtain the operating system Jobs' team developed. Steve Jobs returned to Apple as an adviser, but then was appointed "interim" CEO after Amelio was pushed out. Within a couple of years, Apple returned to profitability and unveiled the iMac, a blue-and-white computer and monitor in one that set Apple on the path to its comeback. It was in 2000 that Apple removed "interim" label from Jobs' CEO title.

The first iPod went on sale in 2001, as did computers with OS X, the modern Mac operating system based on Next software. Apple launched the iTunes music store in 2003 with 200,000 songs at 99 cents each, giving people a convenient way to buy music legally online. It sold 1 million songs in the first week.

Pixar eventually merged with Walt Disney in 2006, and Jobs became the highest stakeholder.

By 2007, Apple was debt-free, and had a reported eighteen billion dollars in the bank. Apple's new generation of customers download its iTunes, and use the iPhone, iPod, and MacBook. The company was named "America's Most Admired Company" (2008 -2011 inclusive), and placed first in the category for "Returns to Shareholders". This is a great achievement as companies that favour shareholders generally do so at the expense of the products or employees. The late Jobs however, was able to maintain shareholder earnings, create successful brands and keep a happy work force what a legacy to follow!

6 Bill Gates

His incredible talent in computing and business have today rewarded him, as he is one of the richest people in the world. Gates now devotes his time to the Bill & Melinda Gates Foundation, which he and his wife founded in 1999. His talent and credibility has enabled his charity to benefit from the legacy of Warren Buffet, who in July 2006 announced that the Foundation would be the recipient of billions of his dollars.

Born William Henry Gates III in 1955, Bill devoured books and excelled in school, although he found it boring and somewhat beneath his abilities. Fearing that their son might become a loner, his parents enrolled him in a private prep school, so that he could broaden his interests and meet the challenges that could help motivate him. One of the most fascinating facts to learn about Bill Gates is the fact that he did not graduate from college or university.

Not only was Gates a wizzard at computer programming, but his talent for business also emerged very early in life. When he was a mere fifteen year old, he and a friend created a software application that earned the two of them twenty-thousand dollars. Gates almost had perfect SAT results, and was guaranteed a place at Harvard, where he enrolled and remained for two years. However, once he experienced success with yet another successful computer program that provided him and his friend with royalties, the taste of success was too much of a distraction. He and Paul Allen formed a company called "Micro-Soft", which meant "micro-computer software". Within a year, the hyphen was deleted, and Microsoft was created.

Gates would now take a key step in his life and career as he realised the need for piracy laws and the protection of innovation. It was this appreciation that would eventually launch Microsoft into the world stage, making its name as recognizable as the word McDonalds. Gates smartly realized that the royalties on his software were very poor and for good reason he wanted to know why. He found that most people just "stole" the applications, as though they were intended for free distribution. He was so frustrated by the practice that he wrote an open letter setting out the reasons why innovation would be stunted if people continued with these same attitudes and bad behaviour.

By 1978, when Gates was twenty-three, he made himself the CEO of Microsoft. He employed twenty-five people and saw the company gross two-and-a-half million dollars. In 1980, Gates started work on a program for the IBM PC. When it was time to sell the source code to IBM, he held back, preferring instead to sell them licenses. Because he had the foresight to protect his property by selling user rights, instead of the code itself, he made billions of dollars over the years through Microsoft. From that point on, the company continued to grow exponentially in turnover, employees, and global recognition.

In 1985, in another defining moment, Microsoft launched Windows, which has become synonymous with Gates. Incredibly, he has been able to create a product that brings computers to the world. Microsoft eliminated the need to use large mainframes and the need to learn a computer language. Anyone could use a friendly computer. Then, in 1987 Gates become a billionaire when Microsoft went public in 1987.

It is right to say that Microsoft has greatly impacted the way many of us live our daily lives from the time we spend in the office to time relaxing on our PCs at home. This is huge!

7 Muhammad Yunus

Muhammad Yunus is a preeminent pioneer who

has encouraged and enabled others to start their own businesses! Microloans from Grameen Bank have helped thousands of poor Bangladeshi women lift themselves from destitution. Bangladesh's Muhammad Yunus and the bank he founded, Grameen Bank, created a new category of banking by granting millions of small loans to poor people with no security - helping to establish the microcredit movement across the developing world. He won the Nobel Peace Prize in 2006. On its Web site, the Norwegian Nobel Committee said it awarded the prize to Yunus and the bank "for their efforts to create economic and social benefit from below."

As a young economics professor at Chittagong University in Bangladesh in 1976, Muhammad Yunus lent $27 out of his money to a group of poor artisans in the nearby town of Jobra. To improve the impact of that "micro" loan, he volunteered to serve as guarantor on a larger loan from a traditional bank, forming the idea for a village-based enterprise named the Grameen Project. It did not occur to the professor that his gesture would inspire a whole category of lending and drive him to the top of a powerful financial institution.

The bank was built on Yunus' conviction that poor people can be both reliable borrowers and avid entrepreneurs. Under Yunus, Grameen has spread the idea of microcredit throughout Bangladesh, Southern Asia, and the rest of the developing world.

When Yunus started Grameen, he planned to turn traditional banking on its head. One of his first moves was to target women, as they are most likely to consider the needs of the family. This was a radical move in a traditional Muslim society, and it took Yunus six years to attain his first target of a 50-50 gender distribution among borrowers. "If banks made large loans, he made small loans. If banks required paperwork, his loans were for the illiterate. Whatever banks did, he did the opposite," marvels Sam Daley-Harris, director of the Microcredit Summit Campaign. "He's a genius."

Yunus then formed a joint venture with food company Dannon to provide nutritionally enhanced yoghurt to poor Bangladeshi children. This type of business allows a company to recoup money invested but not take any dividend beyond that point. Yunus said, "Corporate law in many countries requires companies to maximise profit for shareholders, who can sue the company". "In that system how can you create a social business? We agreed a 50/50 joint venture with Dannon in which they would pay 500,000, but their lawyers advised them that you cannot invest money in a company that will not give you a dividend." Dannon had to write to shareholders to get approval for them to contribute part of the dividend money. Ninety-eight percent agreed and Dannon raised 35 million Euros which they put into a social business fund.

In a recent event called "Lawyers Against Poverty", he debated for the easing of the obligation on public company directors to maximise profits for shareholders. He argued that this would foster the creation of "social business" which can pursue anti-poverty objectives such as providing housing and health care.

Mohammad Yunus is also one of the founding members of Global Elders. Chaired by Archbishop Desmond Tutu, The Elders are an independent group of global leaders who work together for peace and human rights. The team was put together in 2007 by Nelson Mandela, who no longer is an active member of the group but is still an Honorary Elder. The concept originates from a conversation between the entrepreneur Richard Branson and the musician Peter Gabriel. The idea they discussed was simple. There are plenty of communities that look to their elders for guidance or to help solve disputes.

Richard Branson and Peter Gabriel took their idea of a group of 'global elders' to Nelson Mandela, who supported it. With the help of Graça Machel (wife of Nelson Mandela) and Archbishop Desmond Tutu, Nelson Mandela set about bringing the Elders together and formally launched the group in Johannesburg in July 2007.

8 Warren Buffet

'The Oracle of Omaha', has over 60 years amassed a fortune of over $46bn solely from investments.

Buffett's investment company, Berkshire Hathaway, of which he is still chairperson, has more than $2bn in shares. This is thanks to Buffett's strategy of investing in undervalued companies with low overhead costs and high growth potential.

Businessman and investor Warren Buffett was born on August 30, 1930, in Omaha, Nebraska. Like many other hugely successful entrepreneurs, he was something of a genius as a child. Buffett's was strong with figures, and he was capable of adding up numerous columns of numbers right in his head. Investing by age 11, Buffett was running a small business at the age of 13. Buffett later launched the firm Buffett Partnership in Omaha, with great success. In addition to his earnings from the paper route, he also sold racing tip sheets that he made and, by understanding accounting principles, used his bicycle as a way of reducing his tax liability. During his high school years, he persisted in finding different opportunities to earn an income. One of his more profitable enterprises was three pinball machines that were located around town and eventually sold at a profit.

As an entrepreneurial teenager, Buffett bought his first shares with savings from his two paper routes. After investing money for friends in Omaha and continually beating the Dow Jones Average by vast margins, he eventually set up his own company, Berkshire Hathaway, which is named after a textile mill he acquired in 1962.

Recently, Buffet made the biggest philanthropic donation of all time by donating $40bn, 85% of his personal fortune, to the Bill and Melinda Gates Foundation.

QUOTES

"You are neither right nor wrong because the crowd disagrees with you. You are right because your data and reasoning are right."

– Warren Buffett

"Someone's sitting in the shade today because someone planted a tree a long time ago."

– Warren Buffett

Buffet had an innate talent in choosing the undervalued stocks of solid companies. It was not long before people recognized Buffett's success, and began seeking his advice regarding investments. He was also honest in how he did business, as he used the interest rate on government bonds as his earnings' indicator. He didn't charge a fee if his investments did not exceed the going rate of the bonds, and only made a return when his clients achieved financially. After about thirteen years, Buffett felt that he could not progress with Buffett Partnerships, and decided to look out for new opportunities.

Although Buffett Partnerships Limited made him rich (twenty-five million dollars when the partnership was dissolved), it is not how he acquired the bulk of his wealth. Instead, it was from being the CEO and largest shareholder in Berkshire Hathaway Holdings, which is the most profitable investment firm in history. The origin of the firm dates to when Buffett and an associate looked at purchasing a defunct milling operation. When he eventually took over the business, it evolved into the holding company that was the foundation for his future success.

He is the only person to reach the position of one of the richest people in the US by investing in equities. The way in which he acquired Berkshire Hathaway is the blueprint to his business model; look for undervalued companies and seek controlling interest.

Warren Buffett may be one of the richest men in the world, yet one of his favourite meals is hamburgers and Coke. To this day, he continues to live in the same house that he first purchased for just over thirty-one thousand dollars, and has one car. He believes in spending wisely, and definitely does not believe in showing off through possessions.

Buffett is renowned for finding businesses with "a competitive moat" which allows them to grow quickly in the marketplace for a long time and protected from competition.

Coca Cola is one of the best examples in the Berkshire

portfolio. It is an iconic and powerful brand, which make it very difficult for any other players attempting to encroach on Coca Cola's turf. Virgin failed with Virgin Cola and Pepsi has failed to make much of an impression despite actually tasting better than Coke (as found to be the case by various studies and the findings of which form the centre piece of the Pepsi Challenge adverts). As for technology there is Apple, where product quality and brand seem to reinforce each other, creating loyal fans that virtually lock out other competition in the market, and Google, where core intellectual property led to a better user experience, which led the company to dominate the search engine marketplace.

Play the long game and stick to your vision, even if it is out of style. Buffett reminds us that the key to his success has been to focus on investments in "productive assets," those companies that can develop without the need for significant capital investment. These companies efficiently deliver goods and services that are always in demand, through good times and bad.

9 Larry Page and Sergey Brin

Larry Page and Sergey Brin started working together as Stanford computer science graduate students. They created an Internet search engine called BackRub, which ran on Stanford servers for over a year, until Stanford decided that the site was taking up too much bandwidth.

Page and Brin thought that they had invented a system that was quicker and more user friendly than anything available, but when they pitched their invention at AltaVista, Excite, Yahoo! and the other players of cyberspace, there were no takers.

Although Yahoo declined to invest in the new search engine, that company's founder advised Larry Page and Sergey Brin to give up their studies and develop their idea as a business. On September 4, 1998, they officially incorporated the company *Google Inc.* at a friend's garage in California. The Google search engine was revolutionary because it ranked results by the number of links it had to relevant pages, not just the number of times the words showed up on the site. In 2000, Google announced the first billion-URL index, becoming the world's largest search engine.

They changed the name of the site to Google, a play on the mathematical term *googol* a term represented by the numeral one followed by 100 zeros-a reflection of their mission to organize the seemingly infinite amount of information on the Internet.

Today, the company is valued at around 200 billion dollars and employs over 54,000 people worldwide. In the space of 14 short years, the term 'Google' has become so ingrained within the world of the Internet that it has even entered the English language as the verb 'to Google'.

Following this came a string of changes, acquisitions, and much more including the introduction of the Gmail email service, acquisition of Blogger and Youtube, etc. Google went public in August 2004. It expanded to the smartphone market with the acquisition of Android Inc. and launched Google+ its social network.

From the outset, the company has branded itself as a fun place to work. Staff facilities in the Googleplex includes a gym, a piano, a free laundry service, two pools, a volleyball court, more than 9 restaurants and a dinosaur skeleton. On several occasions, Fortune magazine has praised Google as the best workplace in the world. In keeping with the company's declared ethos of promoting fun, staff is actively encouraged to observe April Fool's Day each year. In 2000, Google announced that it had developed a new search method called the MentalPlex, which read the user's brainwaves and removed the need to use the keypad.

In 2001, staff were tasked with the specific job of finding a motto that expressed the company's values. One of them, Amit Patel, recalled that the think-tank quickly became bogged down with slogans, from the specific "Be In Time For Meetings", to the aspirational "Treat Everyone With Respect". Amit said, "Some of us were very anti-corporate and we didn't like the idea of all these specific rules." At this point, one executive, Paul Buchheit, intervened and said, "All of these things can be covered with the three words 'Don't Be Evil'."

Page and Brin seized on the three words and used "Don't Be Evil" to brand Google as one of the "good guys" of the corporate world. The company pledges one percent of its annual profits to a range of projects, ranging from the development of clean energy sources to the provision of healthcare in the Third World.

Larry Page's interest in technology was fuelled at the age of six, when his father, the late Carl Page--Michigan State professor and pioneer in the fields of computer science and artificial intelligence gave him a computer. Page graduated with honors from the University of Michigan with a bachelor's degree in engineering with a focus on computer engineering. He undergraduate claim to fame was that he built an inkjet printer out of Lego blocks.

Page worked for a few years in the technology industry before deciding, aged of 24, to apply for a Ph.D. in computer science at Stanford University. It was there that he met Sergey Brin, who was picked to show him around the university. Brin, left Moscow at the age of six and moved to the U.S. with his family. He received his bachelor's degree in maths and computer science, with honors, from the University of Maryland, which was the same university where his father taught maths. At Stanford, he studied ways to extract patterns and relationships from large amounts of data.

In 1996, Brin joined Page in his BackRub research project, investigating backlinks, which were links on other websites that refer back to a given webpage as a way to measure the relative importance of a particular site. They then developed the PageRank algorithm (named after Page), hypothesizing that by implementing this tool, they could produce better results than existing search engines, which returned rankings based on the number of times a search term appeared.

They tested the BackRub search engine on Stanford's servers. Without a web developer, they maintained a simple search page, but were challenged to find the necessary computing power to handle queries as the search engine became increasingly popular. The two ran the operation out of their dorm rooms as they continued with their studies.

In August 2004, Google went public with an IPO that raised $1.67 billion and became the first and only company to allocate its stocks using computers rather than Wall Street bankers. For the quarter ending June 30, 2008, Google reported turnover of $5.37 billion, an increase of 39 percent compared to the second quarter of 2007.

The company has had a huge impact on the internet, businesses and on the evolution of the information age in our culture and society. Information, products and services have become readily available to everyone!

10 Sir Richard Branson

When asked what it was that helped him become successful in the early stages of his life, the answer he has given is "The art of delegation early in life, and the ability to...find others who are better at doing things than you..."

"That gave me the time to step aside and focus on the entrepreneurial aspect of what I wanted to do. If you have somebody to do the nitty gritty you can focus on the bigger picture."

Sir Richard has always been a people person, and it is that ability to judge and relate to people that ensured he had the right people in his businesses from the start, making it easier for him to think outside of the box without the worries of the day-to-day running of his businesses.

"Give people freedom, let them make mistakes, to get the best out of your staff. Lots of delegation and leave people to get on. Some things they will do differently to you, and better, and some not as good. It can be hard to let go and trust in others, but if you have the right people it becomes a lot easier to step back."

Over a period of 40 years, The Virgin Group has included companies that have embraced air travel, broadcasting, publishing and mobile communications. It is now looking to go in to space and has over 350 companies within the group and its very own island called Necker Island. Necker Island is a 74-acre island in the British Virgin Islands just north of Virgin Gorda – genius!

Now Sir Richard devotes much of his time to personal passions like The Elders, the international human rights group chaired by Archbishop Desmond Tutu.

He has always done things a bit differently. It is a philosophy that is central to the Virgin brand and ethos, and it is the catalyst behind the project he calls "the most exciting thing" the company has ever pursued, Virgin Galactic, the commercial aerospace business devoted to providing spaceflights to private citizens. Passenger service flights are planned to begin by the year's end and it is reported that Virgin Galactic has already signed up around 500 customers willing to pay over $200,000 each to reach an altitude of about 68 miles above the Earth's surface.

According to Branson, "First we're taking people to suborbital space travel, then orbital, and then we'll be able to put satellites into space at a fraction of the price it currently costs. One day, maybe even hotels in space--who's to know?" "Whatever happens, it is going to be ridiculously exciting. It's the start of a whole new era."

Branson built the Virgin Group brand by targeting business verticals "where things are not being run well by other people," and he remains driven by a compulsive desire to do things the way he believes they should be done. Interestingly all of Branson's stories of entrepreneurial success begin as tales of consumer discontent. In the case of Virgin Records, Branson launched his own label because no established company would agree to release multi-instrumentalist Mike Oldfield's hypnotic Tubular Bells; the album inaugurated the Virgin imprint in 1973 and went on to sell more than 16 million copies worldwide.

As for Virgin Atlantic, Branson and 50 other passengers found themselves stranded in Puerto Rico when American Airlines cancelled a flight to the Virgin Islands. He chartered a 50-seat plane, sold each ticket for $39 and not long after Purchased a second hand 747 to launch his airline.

"There is no point in going into a business unless you can make a radical difference in other people's lives," Branson says. "To me, it's like painting a picture: You have to get all the colours right and all the little nuances right to create the perfect picture, or the perfect company. I know that there's need for Virgin to come in and attack a marketplace, because I know that I'm frustrated by having to experience bad service in that particular marketplace."

"So, I'll throw all the paint up and get all the best people in. By the time it sticks on the canvas, we'll try to start getting some order into it. Every little single detail has to be right."

Branson says, "All startups should be thinking, what frustrates me and how can I make it better?" "It might be a small thing or it might be a big thing, but that's the best way for them to think. If they think like that, they're likely to build a very successful business."

Chapter 3

Personality Traits that all great entrepreneurs exhibit

Fearless

Business is not for the faint hearted. You have to have the guts to take the plunge and leave what you are doing and to jump in to new territory. Bill Gates and Mark Zuckerberg quit Harvard, Jeff Bezos left a highly paid job at D.E. Shaw, drove cross-country to Seattle and launched a bookstore out of a garage. Steve Jobs left Stanford and started Apple out of his garage. This drive and instinct are often found in the greatest of entrepreneurs.

Being an entrepreneur requires a certain amount of fearlessness to chase after a dream, especially after setbacks. Setbacks for the greatest entrepreneurs are stepping-stones for opportunity and great life experiences for learning. Branson says he learns most from his failures.

Being fearless the entrepreneur is better able to tackle the many inevitable hurdles on the path to success. Starting almost any business is risky, even if it is a calculated risk. They are non-stop go-getters. They are constantly thinking one-step ahead and rarely end up on the losing side of things.

In *Young Guns: The Fearless Entrepreneur's Guide to Chasing Your Dreams and Breaking Out on Your Own* (AMACOM, 2009), Robert Tuchman shows professionals that they can start and succeed as business owners, with examples of many entrepreneurs below the age of 35. He professes that the best time to take a chance is when people are young, bold full of energy and have very little to lose as he talks from experience.

When Tuchman graduated from college, he was forced to give up his dream of becoming a sportswriter since all his applications to sports programs were ignored. Eventually he took on the position as a trainee stockbroker, but soon realized that he was completely unsatisfied in his new job. He longed for a better job. Tired of working in a job with hardly any prospect of career progression, he formed his own company, Tuchman Sports Enterprises (TSE). Within two years of working out of his tiny one-bedroom Upper East Side Manhattan apartment, with one telephone and a fax machine, his company was named in the annual Inc. Magazine's 500 list of America's fastest growing privately held companies and as one of the top 100 promotion agencies by Promo Magazine. He launched TSE with no money and no investors and ended up selling it for millions of dollars to a major firm.

Desire and perseverance

People who continually succeed are insanely driven. As with sports, it is not enough to be driven. You need to be driven by the right motives and you need to have ability to learn quickly.

"Some people want it to happen, some wish it to happen, others make it happen." Michael Jordan

People that are driven to pursue poor business ideas all the time end up failing. Those that have the desire to pick themselves up learn from their mistakes and move forward in a positive fashion are the successful ones. Most great entrepreneurs are not primarily driven by money. In fact, most of them would probably tell you that money is not even in their top five most important accomplishments.

Most of the greats are driven primarily by the desire to be the best. As an entrepreneur, you must know in your heart that nothing will stop you. You must believe with every ounce of your being that you will not fail and you will not give up. Every day is a new opportunity to get out there and shine. Despite the obstacles that life may throw in your path, you will continue to move forward!

Rocky Balboa said: "It ain't about how hard you hit. It's about how hard you can get hit, and keep moving forward."

An essential attribute of a successful entrepreneur is the ability to forge on in the face of adversity. Nothing can be achieved without hardship. When you think of persistence think of Ray Kroc who worked until his 50s before he saw great success with McDonalds.

He said "Nothing in the world can take the place of persistence. Nothing is more common than unsuccessful men with talent. The world is full with educated derelicts. Persistence and determination alone are omnipotent."

Passion

All entrepreneurs are very passionate about what they do. They rarely quit working even when seemingly engaged in other activities. That passion is what drives them to the incredible desire to swim against the current and come up with fresh new ideas and perspectives that can catapult their business into rapid success. While other people dream about what they will do when they retire, the entrepreneur dreams about how they can improve their product. While other people stand around waiting for it to be time to quit, the entrepreneur wishes there were more hours in the day to work. For example, Part of Richard Branson's passion lies in his zeal for starting companies. Founded in 1970, today the Virgin Group has expanded to more than 400 companies. Branson is famous for his adventurous personality and one of the most admired entrepreneurs for his ability to have a successful work/life balance.

Having a big dream is great, but if people don't have the passion for what they are doing, their dreams will disappear very quickly. If people do not have a passion for what they are doing, it shows in who they are. People are drawn to people with a passion. Passion cannot be faked. People with a passion do not have to pursue others and try to convince them how great what they are doing is. People can read and appreciate this as they feel their passion and it is infectious.

Passionate entrepreneurs have a look of honest excitement and happiness in their eyes, in their body language and in their tone when they interact with their clients, customers, investors, and others. Whether it is the way they talk about their product or discuss their work, passionate entrepreneurs have an infectious excitement and focus that makes others want to connect and do business with them. Passion cannot be faked or overlooked if you really want to connect with your customers, clients, partners or investors.

Clients, customers, employees, and suppliers can tell very quickly when you are not enjoying or are not "passionate" about your business. The genuine smile that exudes joy and satisfaction just is not there when you are "pretending" to be passionate.

Belief and self-discipline

The first 1-2 years of any business startup requires extreme discipline and commitment. You need to have the willpower to force yourself up every morning, to ensure that you make progress even though you are tired or you do not feel well. You have to have the self-discipline to do what needs to be done, especially in the early days when you will not be supervised by others and when you must be self-motivated.

You have to know you will succeed. You have to tell yourself daily and believe that regardless of whatever unforeseen obstacles are in your route, you will find a solution round and progress forward towards the goal. Doubts may creep in from time to time, but it is necessary to have the confidence to squash those doubts to see yourself through. Visualize where you want to be ultimately and know in your heart that you will achieve it.

Entrepreneurs are constantly driven by goals and the belief that they will be successful. The successful entrepreneur can tell you exactly what their goal is and how they anticipate arriving at the goal. They appreciate the importance of a timeline and will do whatever is necessary to arrive at the target on time and under budget.

Knowledge

Great entrepreneurs understand their business and their industry at an expert higher level. They are able to have hours of discussions with anyone on the most minute details of how their business works and the trends in their industries.

Great entrepreneurs read everything they can get their hands on about their business from books to blogs or seek out a mentor. Knowledge is power, and the knowledge of many is power multiplied. Entrepreneurs surround themselves with people that complement their weaknesses to form strategic partnerships. They seek the advice of other entrepreneurs that have gone before them. They ask great questions that will enable them to dig deeper into a subject. They believe that others are smarter than they are and seek out this advice willingly. They are also very adept at getting to the core of a subject without wasting valuable time.

Many entrepreneurs are not highly educated, while others have doctor's degrees. However, there is one thing all entrepreneurs share in common. They are active learners. They find others that have a deep knowledge of a particular area and learn from them.

The seventh habit in the late great Stephen Covey's best seller '7 Habits Of Highly Effective People' is to "sharpen the saw" which is about re-energizing and renewing yourself to sharpen yourself for the tasks in front of you. Such techniques include exercise and nutrition, reading to improve and to develop yourself, planning, writing, study and meditation.

A desire to be innovative.

Great entrepreneurs have a passionate desire to do things better and to improve their products or service. At times, your industry will change. Your customer base may shift. What is "in" today may not be "in" tomorrow. Great entrepreneurs look to stay ahead of the game. Never stop growing. Never stop looking for ways to improve.

Albert Einstein once gave his views on the importance of imagination:

"Logic will get you from A to B. Imagination will take you everywhere."

Creativity sets you apart from your competitors. Imagination provides you with ideas, which enables you to stand out from the crowd. Thinking outside the box that most people remain locked inside of helps you achieve greatness.

People with imagination are actively thinking about how to improve their project. Entrepreneurs continually look around for ideas to improve their project. Everything links back into their project, which is their baby.

Innovation is defined as exploiting new ideas leading to the creation of a new product, service or process. It is not just the invention of a new idea that is important, but rather "bringing it to market", putting it into practice and exploiting it in a manner that leads to new products, services or systems that adds value or improves quality. This could possibly involve technological transformation and the restructuring of management. Innovation also means exploiting new technology and using out-of-the-box thinking to create new value and to bring about important changes in society.

In order to be termed commercial innovations, new products and services need to be strong enough to withstand the rigorous commercialization processes and into the marketplace. Management expert Peter Drucker said that if an established organization is not able to innovate, it is likely to fall in to decline and finally insolvency. Many organizations are implementing new policy to strengthen their ability to innovate. These companies are creating a dependable operating system for innovation, which is a key indicator of corporate sustainability.

Competition combined with strong demand is a major driver of innovation. Intensity of competition fuels innovation and productivity between businesses. Innovation, besides products and services, also includes new business systems, new processes and new methods of management, which have a great impact on productivity and growth.

Today, we need innovators more than any time before. Every business is feeling the impact of globalization, migration, technological and knowledge revolutions, and climate change issues. Innovation should bring added value.

The economy is composed of businesses. Any small business is integral to the economy and without it our economy would not survive. However, a business must also sustain itself, be able to constantly evolve to fulfill the demands of the marketplace. In every business, it is crucial to be innovative industrious and resourceful.

Entrepreneurship produces financial gain and drives the economy, which justifies the importance of innovation in entrepreneurship. Entrepreneurs could be said to be innovators of the economy as they influence its growth. It is not just the scientists who invent and find solutions. The importance of innovation in entrepreneurship is illustrated when new ways to produce a product or a solution are introduced in a business to keep it competitive and ahead of the game. The next Chapter illustrates the importance of forward thinking and the importance of having a unique selling point to ensure you stay successful in today's very competitive business environment. A service industry can expand with another type of service to fulfill the ever-changing needs of their clients. Producers can develop another product from the raw materials and by-products.

The importance of innovation in entrepreneurship is another key value for the longevity of a business. Entrepreneurs and businesses begin with a need. They see the need within the community and come up with a solution. They grab the opportunity to innovate to make lives more comfortable and these solutions keep evolving.

Innovations contribute to the success of the company. Entrepreneurs, as innovators, see not just one solution to a problem or demand. They continue to generate ideas and do not settle until they come up with multiple solutions. Innovation is so important that companies often see their employees' creativity as a solution. They come up with seminars and training to keep their employees stimulated to create something useful for others and, in turn, for financial gain for the company.

Vision and strategy

Establishing goals is a critical component of success, whether you are entrepreneurial or not. There is power and merit in writing down realistic and specific goals and setting out clearly how you will go about achieving and executing them effectively. The best have a clear vision that they work towards by focusing on clear goals they set themselves and their teams. A large project is always simpler to tackle when you break it down into smaller, more manageable sections. Implement this with discipline and regularly have reviews to see where you are. Success comes by achieving your vision; by adopting the right strategy to ensure you get to where you want to go as efficiently as possible.

The business strategy is the plans, choices and decisions used to guide a company to greater profitability and success.

Chapter 4

Essential factors for business success

Entrepreneurs tend to be known for relying on their gut reactions, instinctive behaviour and sometimes-spontaneous decision making which some might say could be risky. Whilst some decisions need to be taken with lightening speed, the following points are designed to help reduce the risk of failure and to help you stay ahead of the game in today's competitive business world.

There is no room for complacency in today's competitive times. Startups as well as existing businesses need to implement key basics throughout the life cycle of the business. Successful leaders look to continually improve their businesses to ensure continued success.

Analyse

Analyse if there is a market for the product or service you wish to provide. What price will the consumer realistically pay? Be creative and have a unique selling point (USP). Research the market to identify the competition, and establish what the consumer is willing to pay for the product or service. Can you change the product or service to give you an edge over your competition?

More well-known car manufacturers are beginning to build hybrid cars since Nissan and Honda got the ball rolling over a decade ago, including new brands which focus purely on building environmentally friendly automobiles, the most famous being Tesla. High performing and innovative brands need to push the boundaries to stay competitive and attractive in the market and to ensure that the brand promise continues to deliver over time such as Audi and BMW, to name but a few. Now, with more importance being placed on corporate social responsibility and when governments are promoting environmentally friendly initiatives to comply with the Kyoto Protocol, car manufacturers cannot ignore this mood and change in the marketplace and need to evolve accordingly.

Section 172 of the Companies Act 2006 provides that the directors of a company have a duty to promote the success for their company for the benefit of the shareholders as a whole and in so doing have regard to:

i.   The likely consequences of any decision in the long term;

ii. The interests of the company's employees;

iii. The need to foster the company's business relationships with suppliers, customers and others;

iv. The impact of the company's operations on the community and the environment;

v.   The desirability of the community maintaining

reputation for high standards of business conduct; and

vi. The need to act fairly as between members of the company.

Directors need to have regard to these factors. None takes precedence over the others. All need to be considered where relevant, but the overriding obligation is to "promote the success of the company". If the decision is to shut a factory or choose a less environmentally friendly solution, the best option for the company as a whole is the option to be followed, of course subject to observing the relevant rules and regulations in force that apply. If the directors fail to consider these issues when reaching a decision, they run the risk of personal liability for any loss to the company from their breach of duty to promote the success of the company.

Position

Position your product or service effectively within the market by building a strong brand. A brand is a promise, a reputation an image, tagline or perception, which consumers connect with when they see the company logo. A great brand lends a twist and resonance to a product or service.

Your brand is whatever your customers perceive it to be. More often than not, there is a gap between what you think of your brand and how customers, distributors, suppliers and even your employees perceive it. If you do not know how others perceive your brand, then whatever strategy you put in place will be flawed. If you want to know what the consumer perceives your brand have a consultancy carry out a brand audit.

Once you know how your brand is perceived, you can then position your brand more effectively. The branding project you undertake should examine different positioning strategies and the pros and cons of each one. When a positioning strategy is chosen, it needs to be clearly articulated and understood.

A successful brand also needs to deliver on the brand promise. Brand promises have five components:

1. Differentiating yourself, your business or your product from the competition. The who, what and why?
2. Everything must be aligned behind the brand.
3. Innovation is necessary to keep pushing the boundaries and keep ahead.
4. You need to assess what you are doing regularly by researching and listening to customers.
5. Finally, you must evolve and nurture your brand by trying to improve what you do.

Successful organisations create value by building powerful brands. Behind every successful brand lies a clearly defined corporate vision that is consistently expressed through the company's external communications, as well as through its internal business processes. A strong brand is important for increasing sales, strengthening core customers and loyalty, and enhancing business performance.

The real power and meaning behind great brands lie more in their intangible values than in their tangible features. Intangible values refer to things such as customer preferences, loyalty and bonding, your brand's reputation and credibility, the associations and imagery of your brand, the core values behind your brand, and even in employees' loyalty and belief in your brand. These intangible values create an invisible, but strong support network behind your business offerings.

They raise your product's perceived value and, as a result, act to both establish and differentiate the brand from rivals. When one product is more or less the same as another, how can brands stand out from the rest? Here, physical characteristics can only play a superficial part – the bigger role is played by the intangible values of the brand. With branding, an emotional and psychological bond with customers can be established. This is key in maintaining market share in a competitive market. Look at Pepsi and Coke, Starbucks and Costa, McDonalds and Burger King, Audi and BMW and the list can go on. Look at these examples in your own time and analyse how the brands differ for effective positioning in the marketplace.

Companies must work hard to build brands. David Ogilvy insisted: "Any damn fool can put on a deal, but it takes genius, faith and perseverance to create a brand."

The sign of a great brand is how much loyalty or preference it commands. Harley Davidson is a great brand because Harley Davidson motorbike riders rarely switch to another brand. Nor do Apple users want to switch to Microsoft.

A company needs to think about what its brand is supposed to mean. What should Nike mean, Audi mean? A brand must be given a personality. It must thrive on some trait(s) and the traits must spread through all of the company's marketing activities. Live and breathe your brand!

Should you establish a new name for a new product, rather than continue with the company's name? The company name evokes a feeling of more of the same, rather than something new. For example Toyota chose not to call its luxury car Toyota Luxury but instead Lexus; Apple Computer did not call its new computer Apple IV but Macintosh; Levi's did not call its new trousers Levi's Cottons but Dockers; Sony did not call its new videogame Sony Videogame but PlayStation. Creating a new brand name gives more opportunity to establish and circulate a fresh public relations story to gain valuable attention and discussion in the media. A new brand needs credibility, and PR is much better than advertising in establishing credibility.

However, every rule has its exceptions. Mr Branson has put the name Virgin on many businesses, including Virgin Atlantic Airways, Virgin Holidays, Virgin Trains, Virgin Limousines, and Virgin Radio, Virgin Publishing. A company needs to ask: How far can the brand name be stretched before it loses its meaning after all Virgin Cola didn't work!

Aim

Aim to have your business running like a well-oiled machine. Pick the right teams, ensure that they are managed and motivated well with effective communication. Adopt the right technology.

Creating the right teams is key to your business success. Team members need to communicate well with one another and gel to become creative and productive.

Picking the right team generally will be within the remit of Human Resources (HR). Whilst at the start up stage the founding directors usually get involved with all areas, allocating specific areas of responsibility should be the preferred way of running the business to help avoid conflicts and to promote a sense of responsibility.

Promoting interaction and communication is key to creativity. The late Steve Jobs believed that interaction equalled innovation. He knew that innovation and creativity do not happen in cubes or through email. According to the Pixar designer and Academy Award winning director (The Incredibles and Ratatouille) Brad Bird describes the Pixar building that Jobs created:

"Steve put the mailboxes, the meeting rooms, the cafeteria, and, most insidiously and brilliantly, the bathrooms in the centre-which initially drove us crazy-so that you run in to everybody during the course of a day. (Jobs) realised that when people run in to each other,

when they make eye contact things happen. So he made it impossible for you not to run in to the rest of the company".

Nurture the right culture for your business. It directly affects the creation and direction of your brand. The culture of a business is the values and practices shared by the staff. These change over time as staff come and go. The easiest way to assess your company's culture is to look around, how do employees act? What do they do? Look for common behaviours. Listen to your employees, note what is written about your company, including on the internet. These will give you a better picture as to what your company's culture really is.

Before you can change the company culture, you need

to decide what you want the company culture to look like in the future. Consider what kind of culture will work best with your organization in its desired future state. Review your mission, vision and values and make sure the company culture you are designing supports them.

Some examples of characteristics of company cultures include:

1. Mission clarity
2. Employee commitment
3. High integrity workplace
4. Strong trust relationships.
5. Promotion and support for innovation
6. Customer or client focused

The right culture is essential, as it will fuel the business in the right direction. You therefore need to align your company culture with your strategic goals if it is not already. Know where you want to go, pick the right team and nurture the right culture to get there!

Cash flow

Improve cash flow by increasing turnover and reducing costs. Implement the right marketing strategy.

Expenses associated with administering a business on a day-to-day basis are operating costs, which include both fixed costs and variable costs. Fixed costs are ones that do not vary with sales. For example, rent paid on a business premises. The rent stays the same whether or not sales of goods in the shop increases or decreases.

Variable costs, such as materials, can vary according to how much product is produced. Variable costs vary with sales. For example, a retailer purchases Marmite from the wholesaler for an average price of 60p per jar. It then sells for a higher price. For the retailer, the variable cost is 60p per jar. It increases and decreases in proportion to changes in sales or production level. Variable costs mainly remain the same per unit or product, or per unit of activity. Additional units manufactured or sold cause variable costs to increase. As the number of units manufactured or sold decrease it results in variable costs going down.

Budgeting for costs when starting up is important to set you on the right path. Budgeting is important when preparing a business plan for a startup. Analyse and incorporate realistic costs in order to give you a realistic profit projection.

The information age has made it a lot easier for companies to market their business. No longer do you just have to spend large sums on advertising in the newspapers. Social media, email, website and SEO are methods of marketing that allow SMEs to compete with the bigger businesses. With this technology evolution, marketing costs can be cut, whilst effectively reaching out to a target audience with effective messaging to connect with clients or customers.

Engage

Engage with your customers and clients so that you can build a strong positive following. In this very competitive business environment, it is essential that you do not forget clients or consumers after they have purchased from you. With their consent, take their contact details and send them useful information in the form of newsletters or emails about how your business can be of continued service to them. Blogs and social media provide different methods of engaging with and communicating with your customers. Facebook works best when businesses are looking to sell to consumers, whilst Twitter and LinkedIn works best for selling to other businesses. Educate, communicate and engage with your target audience online.

Twitter is a very effective way of communicating with the world. Each tweet consists of no more than 140 characters in which you should send out golden nuggets of information that would be of interest to your potential target audience. Your tweets should tell the world about your business which in turn could help build your name and brand.

Effective engagement is all about building a strong long-term relationship with your customer/client base. The first experience you give your client should be a wow experience to hook them and make sure they go away very pleased and likely to refer and return. A wow experience is one where the business goes the extra mile and delivers. For example, a special/unique look feel in a retail outlet, delivery of high level of service combined with technology for ease in the service sector. Once you have "delivered", wowed customers are more likely to give you their details to stay in touch.

Whichever method of engagement you use, whether it is Twitter or blogging, it is important to create interesting pieces that are informative and useful to start creating the engagement you are looking for. Master one before you dabble in all methods.

Partner

Partner with like-minded organisations or individuals to help position your business more definitively.

Creating synergistic relationships is becoming more and more common where companies draw on the brand strength, influence and talent others have established for a win/win outcome.

The most important and impactful brands are those that have put competition behind them and embraced collaboration as an operating principle. These brands are clear about their ambitions and are not shy about seeking out others who share those ambitions. It is with these partners they will pool resources to create a better future.

Look at McDonalds and BMW, the main brand partner sponsors of the Olympics 2012. The Olympics is arguably the greatest sporting event in the world, bringing together athletes from all the corners of the world to compete. I could not believe the number of BMWs that were used do drive stars, sports people, the press etc. when we spent a day at Wimbledon during the Olympics. It is a win/win partnership.

In January 2007, Volvo Cars and Vattenfall launched the industrial partnership, with the aim to test and develop plug-in technology. Vattenfall operates a commercial energy business attempting to be among the leaders in developing environmentally sustainable energy production. One of the results of this cross-border initiative was the formation of a jointly owned company, V2 Plug-in-Hybrid Vehicle Partnership. It has led to the creation of The Volvo V60 Plug-in Hybrid that was presented in March, at the 2011 Geneva Motor Show with production starting in the autumn of 2012; the world's first diesel plug-in hybrid.

Volvo Cars' President Stefan Jacoby has been quoted as saying, "No single industry or organisation can tackle the climate challenge on its own. It is Volvo's mission to develop carbon dioxide-lean cars, but everyone concerned must build up a sustainable future jointly. This project shows how cooperation between experts in different areas takes us one step closer from individually carbon dioxide-lean products to a well-thought-out climate-smart lifestyle."

Cisco's highly ambitious Cisco I-Prize innovation contest invited outsiders to develop a business plan that took Cisco into territories they had not explored before. The winning entry was put to the company's own executives, and Cisco handed the victor $250,000. The plan consisted of household devices such as toasters and dishwashers that could tell the electricity grid what their energy usage is likely to be before being turned on. This would allow the grid to manage energy requirements in the same way that Internet infrastructure manages the demands of server traffic.

Could Cisco have conceived this idea? Possibly, but it did not. The energy-saving initiative has gone into development, and Cisco has created a great pool of new ideas which contains the remaining 1,000 unsuccessful business-plan entries.

This is a smarter way of doing business. In this world of collaboration, brands need to get smarter about how they behave. The most impactful see themselves as performers on a wider stage, as having to understand and interact with the other performers on the same stage.

Brand domination will be a strategy of the past. The brands of the future will work with others to further their ambitions, with shared outcomes and incentives, and a culture of approachability.

The concept of partnering is not just relevant in the context of brand building, but at all levels of business; when starting a business, expanding or when picking the team within the organisation. As can be seen in Chapter 2, even the greatest entrepreneurs did not achieve success on their own - they had great partners.

SS Business Consultants Limited has partnered with John Warrillow, best-selling author of Built to Sell and SME expert, to give clients their Sellability Score. This can be accessed via our website. The online tool provides a free 26-page report on the current position of your business and ways of improving its value to ensure a successful future.

I first saw Raymond Aaron at Business 2012 at the O2 Arena when he took the stage after Richard Branson. Impressively, he managed to keep me from leaving to see Richard Branson's planned appearance in the nightclub next door. I very quickly saw what positive impact he could have on my brand and soaked up what he had to say and enrolled on his 10:10:10 course for writing a book.

Be forward thinking.

By being forward thinking, I do not mean predict the future. I mean think ahead and plan.

Do not work mindlessly without having an end game in mind. Work to achieve your goal by regularly reviewing and evaluating and making necessary changes to make sure you are still on course.

If you plan and make necessary changes, you are less likely to run the risk of unforeseen challenges and obstacles that may appear in the future. You may need to buy new technology. Do not ignore it. Plan so that you can budget for it; think how your business in the future will best require the technology to ensure best performance. How might the market want your product to be different? Will culture changes in the future affect your service or product? Try to anticipate how the market will change for your product or service.

Keep abreast of the news and the continual changes around you; think about its impact and act accordingly.

Chapter 5

How to acquire a property for as little as £1

Property remains a favourite investment to have in your portfolio, especially for entrepreneurs. It is an asset you can see, touch and work your creative flair on to unlock its potential; whether it be a capital gain by marking it up after purchase and selling it or looking also for rental income and capital gain over time.

Raising finance today is not easy, especially if you have a bad credit rating or do not qualify for the strict criteria required by institutional lenders. Those in the property "game" look to purchase jointly with trusted joint venture partners if they cannot afford a property on their own. Alternatively, they can look to purchase using instalment contracts.

Instalment contracts are a creative tool for generating cash flow and profit without significant upfront payment and finance as required when traditionally purchasing a property. They do not work in all situations, but are powerful if used correctly. This tool was adopted by Australian property guru Rick Otton from the US. As it is relatively less common in the UK it is all the more essential that you seek advice from an experienced lawyer before you enter in to these transactions. You may also find it helpful to retain a creative property agent who is familiar with these transactions to structure a suitable deal for you whether you may be a motivated seller or buyer.

As with all new systems and creations this does have its skeptics. There is one school of thought that believes that what is described below falls within regulated activity under the FSA regulations which means that only a suitably regulated financial adviser can advise the motivated buyer on the deal. It is a matter of interpretation which is open for debate and would welcome clear guidance from the FSA.

A traditional conveyance of property generally requires a 10% deposit from the buyer on exchange of contracts followed by the balance of the agreed purchase price on completion. However where appropriate, a creative tool to purchase property can instead be used by the buyer/ investor such as an option to purchase, for say the duration of the remaining mortgage, on the property for a £1 rather than exchange with a 10% deposit. The buyer/investor, at the same time, completes on a management agreement with the seller, which sets out the rights and obligations for both parties for the use of the property during the term of the option. A Power of Attorney is also granted to enable the buyer to fully enjoy the use of the property as though he/she were the owner.

The buyer/investor "babysits" the existing mortgage and all other outgoings on the property during the option period, and therefore needs to have the legal authority under the Power to be able to deal with all legal issues relating to the property.

Case Study

John is looking to sell his three bedroom terraced house in Barnet North London. It has been on the market for over 9 months. The property was on initially for £230,000, however John needs to sell quickly due to financial difficulty, as he is finding it hard to keep up with his mortgage payments. John does not want a quick sale for £200,000, as there will be no equity for him.

There is a mortgage amount of £200,000 secured against the property for a term of 15 years at a rate of 3.5% interest equating to £583.33 monthly interest payments.

Sarah, a prospective purchaser, agrees to take an option to purchase within the 15-year period at a price of £232,000 with an exchange deposit of £1, which will release John from having to pay monthly mortgage payments. Sarah will have the period of 15 years (the term of the mortgage) to exercise the option to purchase. This affords Sarah flexibility, enabling her to think about what she wants to achieve from the property and plan her exit strategy. For example, she can:

i. exercise the option to purchase in, say, two years, having let it out (which generates positive cash flow during this time, assuming the rent is higher than the mortgage payments of £583.33) and thereby generating a positive cash flow as soon as she finds a tenant; and,

ii.   decorate the property to increase its value, e.g. put in a kitchen and then let for a higher rent or find a buyer or exercise the option to purchase.

What happens if Sarah wants to find a buyer with a view to making increased cash flow profit on exchange and further profit on completion?

This is where Sarah can secure a prospective purchaser with an instalment contract. This will allow a buyer who is looking to buy a property to enter on to the property ladder without initially having to secure a mortgage. This is ideal for families who have a sizeable deposit, but do not qualify for a mortgage because they are either unemployed, self-employed or their income is not regular. It also works well for those who are fed up of renting and not getting closer to owning the property they live in. This solution allows the buyer to pay instalments to the buyer/investor, in this example Sarah, with the ability to purchase the property at a fixed date or earlier under the instalment contract.

Sarah finds Mr. & Mrs. Singh who are looking to get on to the ladder. She can provide the Singhs with an instalment contract to buy the property in, say, the 3rd anniversary of the contract date at a price of £250k. It is calculated that the period of 3 years will give them time to be able to find a mortgage. During the three years, Sarah calculates what a bank would receive on a loan of £225k over 25 years with a capital and interest payment of 6.25%. On exchange, the Singhs would give Sarah a 10% deposit of £25,000 leaving £225,000. The monthly mortgage payments would be £1,484.26. Sarah would receive this on a monthly basis until year three or earlier. This provides Sarah positive cash flow of £900.93, once the current monthly mortgage instalment of £853.33 is paid.

The Singhs only move in under an Assured Shorthold Tenancy agreement, once they enter in to the instalment contract with Sarah. The agreement gives certainty to both parties.

Summary

The above tool should be considered and applied with a win/win mindset from the outset. John needed to be relieved from his mortgage payments and secure equity (motivated seller). Sarah saw an opportunity and structured a deal to reward both John and her and assisted the Singhs (motivated buyers) secure the property they liked, which otherwise they could not afford.

There are other scenarios that lend themselves well for instalment contracts. Where there is more significant equity in a property, a deposit of £1 may not be appropriate. It is particularly useful if you are having difficulty selling your property and you do not necessarily need a large deposit to fund a related purchase. You may need a buyer fast because you are finding it hard to meet your mortgage payments or you are looking to get on to the property ladder, but cannot qualify for a mortgage until, say, 2-3 years when you expect your financial situation to improve.

Please treat this Chapter merely as a guide to illustrate how by thinking creatively you can acquire property without a large deposit, or mortgage. The Chapter does not constitute detailed legal advice and certainly does not cover all the issues that need to be presented to the respective parties by their lawyer. Anyone interested in using creative tools for acquiring property must retain an experienced lawyer in this field to ensure that all issues are addressed with transparency and ethically to reduce potential risk for all concerned.

For another useful case study visit www. entrepreneurshipandproperty.com which also sets out the benefits of this tool for the seller, investor and end buyer.

Chapter 6

Key Points to Consider When Purchasing an Investment Property

Are you looking for a quick return or long-term growth and source of income generation? Location influences price, rent and yield. Typically, the value of a property doubles over a period of 8 to 10 years. Rental yield is the amount of money a Landlord receives in rent in the course of one year, shown as a percentage of the sum of money invested in the property. It follows that the higher the yield, the better. Compare the yield with other investment opportunities such as shares, bonds, investing in a startup or other business.

In addition to prime property locations, which are well known for stable and rising property values such as central London, there are Enterprise Zones. According to the Department for Business Innovation and Skills website, Enterprise Zones are specific areas where a combination of reduced planning restrictions, financial incentives and other support is used to encourage the creation of new businesses and jobs – and contribute to the growth of the local and national economies.

Twenty-four Enterprise Zones are already up and running across the country benefiting from:

- a Business Rate discount per company of approximately £275,000 over a five year period;
- a retention, for a minimum of 25 years, of the Business Rate growth from the Zone in order to support the relevant local enterprise partnership's economic priorities;
- Simplified planning, by implementing Local Development Orders;
- Government help to ensure that superfast broadband is integrated throughout each Zone.

There are some Enterprise Zones that benefit from 100% first year capital allowances for plant and machinery.

The internet is a great way of examining comparable property prices and property details before you decide to buy.

Key Costs and related Legal Issues
When Buying a Property

Acquisitions costs are tax deductible, however it is important to get correct tax advice from the start so that you can plan with certainty to ensure you really will be making the profit you project. Typical costs of a purchase can be broken down as follows:

Solicitors' fees generally will depend on the price

of the property and whether the property is freehold or leasehold, whether there is a mortgage and whether the property is residential or commercial. If there is a mortgage, additional work is necessary in advising on the mortgage terms, complying with conditions and reporting to the lender with a clear certificate of title in order to be able to draw down on the funds for completion. The work with a leasehold purchase is typically more involved as there is the lease to read and report on.

Search costs can range from £150 to £450. It is usually the local search that differs in price, depending on the local authority fee. Where a property is funded by a mortgage, the mortgage conditions will require the following searches: the local search, drainage, environmental and chancel. These searches reveal important information relating to the property. The search relates to the property and so additional enquiries may need to be raised to answer questions that impact the neighbourhood. The results reveal important information, which if adverse may negatively affect the value and marketability of the property. If there are onerous entries, they will need to be addressed before contracts can be exchanged so that the lender can agree to lend on the property.

The local search will reveal, for example, the planning and building regulation history of the property. You will be able to find out whether the property has been built with consent from the local authority and, equally, if there is an enforcement notice for a breach, for example of lack of planning/building regulation or listed building consent.

The drainage search will reveal if there is a drain running with the boundary of the property and whether there is build over consent for building over a drain or within 3m from the property. Consent is required where a building is erected within 3m from the drain. Without consent from the appropriate utility company, you will be at risk. The company can knock down parts of the property to access the drain without having to compensate the property owner. This can be avoided if there is build over consent. Alternatively, a suitable build over indemnity policy can be purchased, which is an insurance policy that protects the owner against loss if there is no agreement in place.

Environmental Searches can indicate such things as whether the property is in a flood risk area, whether the property has been built on contaminated land and previous land use.

The chancel search indicates whether the property is in an area of chancel repair liability. The liability relates to the historic responsibility for upkeep of a church being split between the rector and the parishioners. The parishioners' responsibilities were eventually transferred by statute to the church, however the rector's responsibility passed with the sale of the land to future owners. Under the Chancel Repairs Act 1932, a Parochial Church Council (PCC) has the power to serve a demand for the expenses or contributions towards the expenses of repairing the church chancel. If the home owner fails to pay, the PCC can enforce the demand through the courts. The famous House of Lords case of *Aston Cantlow v Wallbank (2003)* illustrated how the PCC successfully enforced its rights to recover the sum of around £450,000 for chancel repair.

Under a 2003 amendment to the Land Registration Act 2002, PCCs must have registered their chancel repair interest against properties at the Land Registry before the 13 October, 2013 if they want to be able to use it. If liability exists but is not registered at the Land Registry, a PCC will be able to enforce it against existing property owners until the property changes hand.

It is essential that your solicitor carries out the right searches and investigates the title by raising appropriate enquiries prior to exchange of contracts.

Land Registry fees depend on the value of the property. Visit the Land Registry Website for useful information. The bankruptcy search against your name is required, especially if you are purchasing with the aid of a mortgage, as it is a requirement of all mortgages. The priority search protects the purchaser and lender from any adverse entries from being entered at the Land Registry, which would rank ahead of the lender's charge until the Transfer in favour of the purchaser is registered at the Land Registry together with the mortgage.

Buyers must pay Stamp Duty Land Tax; the rates can be found in the website of HM Revenue and Customs. You should consult a tax expert who will be able to advise on the most suitable vehicle to purchase your property to ensure that tax is kept legally to a minimum; whether it be to purchase in your name, set up a trust or to set up an alternative corporate entity.

Repair costs are another important factor. Get reliable quotes from recommended builders to ensure you have a realistic budget for the property so that you can achieve your projected return on investment. Do not get carried away and spend as though you will be living there- remember it is only an investment!

Consult an architect to help you cost up the investment

potential of the property. The architect will help you achieve the best use of the property in terms of development potential. You may think it has potential for nine flats whereas the architect may have other creative ideas that can help you achieve a better return. Your architect is the person who puts together the planning application and is in the best position to know whether you are likely to get planning permission for the development. Feedback from an architect and accountant can help you work out if your plans for the property are commercially viable.

Planning Permission

At the time this book is being written, the government has expressed that they would temporarily relax the planning laws for three years in order to help the economy by kick starting construction and related businesses. The government is putting the proposals out to consultation.

Certain works do not require permission because they are classed as Permitted Development. Depending on where you live, conservation areas and listed buildings have different rules; but generally speaking, extensions, loft conversions and conservatories can all be permitted developments. There are however restrictions if you decide to extend your home and the main ones include:

- All extensions and other buildings must not exceed 50% of the total area around the property as it stood on 1 July 1948, or the day it was built, if later.
- The extension must not be on the side of the house that faces the road.
- On a detached property, a single storey extension

can be up to 4m long and side extensions can only be a single storey.

- On a terraced or semi-detached property, a single storey extension can only be 3m long.
- The building must not be covered in any outlandish material – if you want to create something that does not match the exterior of your property you will need to get the council's permission.
- Single storey extensions must not exceed 4m in height.
- two-storey extensions can only be 3m long.

The government's planning portal website has very useful information details on common works that are undertaken on a property, including setting out what constitutes permitted developments. The Communities and Local Government website is also a great source of useful information.

The government's new proposals intend to make the following changes and introductions:

- Relax for up to 3 years the planning rules on extending homes and business premises.
- For a detached home, a single storey extension increase up to 8m long (currently 4m).
- On a terraced or semi-detached home, a single storey extension to be up to 6m long (currently 3m).
- Removing criteria for developers to include affordable housing - if they prove they make a site "commercially unviable".
- An extra £280m for the FirstBuy scheme to help would-be homeowners with a deposit.

- A new bill to provide £40bn in government guarantees to underwrite major infrastructure projects and £10bn to underwrite the construction of new homes.
- Funding of £300m to provide 15,000 affordable homes and bring 5,000 empty homes back into use.
- A new "major infrastructure fast-track" for big projects.
- Placing underperforming council planning departments into "special measures" and allowing developers to bypass them if they fail to improve.
- Businesses to be able to extend shops by 100 square metres and industrial units by 200 square metres.

At the time this book is being written, these proposals have yet to be put into force, merely being consulted upon by government. It is important to be aware of these changes and the current view of government so that you can plan. At all times consult an expert before carrying out work to ensure that you are not in breach of planning and or building regulation, or other relevant regulations which would impact on the marketability of the property. A property investor should have a reliable team of experts to consult, which includes the solicitor, accountant, surveyor, and architect.

Whilst you may not need planning permission if you are building an extension, you may have to comply with the Party Wall Act 1996 and serve a party wall notice on your neighbour at least two months before starting work to the party wall. The adjoining property owner may consent to works starting earlier, but is not legally obliged to even if agreement is reached on the works. The notice is only valid for a year, so it is unwise to serve some time before you plan to start work. Equally, if you want to build up against or astride your neighbours boundary line, the right party wall notice needs to be given this time at least one month before works start, which is only valid for a year. If works are commenced without following the right procedure, your neighbour can stop the work by a court injunction or seek other legal redress to include a claim for any damage to their property.

Extend Short Lease or Purchase of the Freehold?

A lease which has less than 80 years can be purchased at a relatively cheap price compared to a healthy one (90 years plus). Generally, most lenders will not lend on a lease that has less than 70 years. Once the lease term is below the 80-year mark, you will have to pay an additional sum to the market price, which is called the marriage value. It is important to factor in to the deal how much you would be expected to pay to purchase a lease extension once you have completed the purchase.

It is usually cheaper to informally agree to the price of a lease extension or freehold purchase with your landlord once you have obtained a valuation from an experienced valuer, without forcing the issue by serving the appropriate notice.

If you cannot agree the right price with your landlord, then you need to establish whether you are entitled to force a lease extension or can collectively acquire the freehold with your fellow leaseholders in the building.

You will be entitled to a lease extension if you have owned a residential lease for at least two years, giving you an additional 90 years on top of the remaining term with the rent reduced to a peppercorn (nil). Where you are buying a flat with a short lease, it may be advisable to ask the seller to reduce the sale price accordingly and serve a section 42 notice on the landlord to start the lease extension process rolling (assuming that the seller has owned the lease for at least 2 years) and assign the benefit to you so that you can complete the lease extension once the flat purchase is complete. This will avoid the 2-year wait after completion during which time the price of an extension will rise especially if the lease term is below 80 years.

Ask whether the leaseholders are interested in purchasing the freehold of the building It is advisable to contact an experienced surveyor to consider the price of the freehold compared to the price of extending your lease. Factor the number of leaseholders that wish to join in, as costs will be split accordingly.

What are the benefits of owning your freehold and being your own landlord?

1. You can extend your leases without having to pay a premium to the landlord. It is prudent to extend the term to 999 years and reduce the rent to a peppercorn. It is also the right time once you purchase the freehold to address any defects in the lease and update the lease to enhance its marketability.
2. You can appoint your preferred managing agents or manage the building yourself to improve

management if this is an issue. (This is on the assumption that the building does not already have a Residents Management Company where the leaseholders are members for the purpose of managing the building). Alternatively, leaseholders have the right to form a Right to Manage Company (RTM) if the existing managing agents are bad, and take over the control of the management by deciding who manages. Forming an RTM is a cheaper option than acquiring the freehold if your only concern is the management of the building.

3. It can give you greater control in how you use your property. Residential leases can request that leaseholders obtain landlord's consent before:

   a) Alterations are made to the property e.g. installing new windows, extending in to the loft and changing the layout of the flat.

   b) Subletting the whole or part of the property.

   c) Keeping a pet at the flat.

Even after the leaseholder purchases a share of the freehold property, these questions must still be addressed. However, a more practical stance is likely to be taken to improve the enjoyment of the property.

Landlords commit a criminal offence if they sell their freehold without first formally offering it to the leaseholders.

The Energy Act 2011

On Tuesday, 18 October 2011, the Energy Bill received Royal Assent and became the Energy Act 2011.

The Act provides for a change in the provision of

energy efficiency measures to homes and businesses, and makes improvements to secure low-carbon energy supplies and fair competition in the energy markets.

The Act includes provisions relating to the Private Rental Sector and the Green Deal.

The Green Deal is intended to empower consumers by giving them new ways of funding home improvements, and empower businesses by enabling them to compete for energy efficiency opportunities in new and innovative ways. It plans to boost the low carbon economy by supporting many jobs in the insulation sector alone by 2015.

The Green Deal creates a new finance option to enable the provision of fixed improvements to the energy efficiency of households and commercial properties, and is funded by a charge on energy bills that overcomes the need for consumers to pay upfront. Instead of having to take from savings or take out loans to improve insulation, double glazing or perhaps a new boiler, you take out long-term finance that will attach to your home.

Many of these details are being consulted on as the government develops its plans. Solar panels may be available in Green Deal packages, but that is not yet clear. You may be able to purchase the Green Deal from an energy supplier, supermarket or other providers.

Since the 1st October Qualified assessors are able to offer you assessments, but you will not be able to take out a Green Deal finance plan until 28 January 2013. From 28 January, Green Deal Providers will be able to offer Green Deal finance plans of up to £10,000 to consumers and begin delivering energy efficiency and heating measures.

It is the intention that consumers pay back the loan

through their energy bills. Whilst the Department of Energy and Climate Change (DECC) is championing the initiative, it is not a government grant. Consumers who choose to take the Green Deal finance will have to pay the money back to the finance company with interest.

The Green Deal process has four steps: assessment, finance, installation and repayment.

- The Green Deal assessor or advisor will assess your home and recommend energy-saving improvements in a Green Deal advice report.
- The Green Deal provider will then quote for a Green Deal plan to pay for the improvements based on the Green Deal advice report.
- The Green Deal installer will if agreed provide and install the measures under the Green Deal plan.
- Your electricity supplier will pay back the Green Deal 'loan' through the savings made on your electricity bills.

The government is keen to stress that the Green Deal is not a 'loan' in the traditional sense. The theory is that you do not pay back more money than you are saving on your energy bills each month. The DECC call this the 'Golden Rule.'

The Golden Rule provides for example that if your new insulation saves you £15 per month on your heating bills you will pay less than £15 in repayments. Important to note that, the Golden Rule does not guarantee savings, it is an estimate based on assumptions. It means that you could be in a 'break-even' situation for many years with no actual net benefit.

The Green Deal does not work like a personal loan as it encumbers your home rather than you, so it will pass on to the new homeowner when you sell. This could give rise to concern for the consumer, as there is uncertainty as to whether the new homeowner will want to purchase a property with a Green Deal charge attached to it.

The government has suggested that the interest rates could be around the 7-8%. Over a long period of time, this rate of interest will add a significant amount to the cost of the product purchased. You should consider all the implications carefully when signing up to long-term financial arrangements.

The Energy Act includes obligations on the part of private residential landlords that from April 2016, they will be unable to refuse a tenant's reasonable request for consent to energy efficiency improvements where a financing, such as the Green Deal and/or the Energy Company Obligation (ECO), is available.

The Act also provide for powers to ensure that from April 2018, it will be illegal to rent out a residential or business premise that does not reach a minimum energy efficiency standard (the intention is for this to be set at EPC rating 'E').

Green Leases

Green Leases incorporate provisions committing the landlord and the tenant to use a property in a more sustainable way to reduce its negative environmental impact. This may involve, for example, obliging a landlord or tenant to introduce energy efficiency measures.

Generally, Green Leases concern commercial premises but remain relatively uncommon in the UK. In the UK, the CRC Energy Efficiency Scheme was introduced in 2010, which led to the use of Green Leases by the larger institutions.

Whilst the adoption of Green Leases has not been very significant, it will no doubt feature more over time as sustainable initiatives aimed at reducing carbon output and increasing energy efficiency become more and more important on the world scene. The introduction of Green Leases resulted mainly from the EU Energy Performance of Buildings Directive and the UK's targets agreed in the Kyoto Protocol. As the focus on carbon output strengthens and energy prices head only one way, the approach by landlords and tenants in the maintenance and management of properties becomes ever more important, particularly, in the commercial lettings sector.

The obligations in a Green Lease may cover the use of environmental contractors, maintaining Energy Performance Certificates and joint strategies/liaison protocols and tenant handbooks.

In 2009, the Better Buildings Partnership, a group of some of London's leading commercial property owners, published the Green Lease Toolkit to provide a foundation on which parties could work together to improve the sustainability of their property. It is unfortunate that despite all of these announcements and initiatives, the property sector has not seen green lease provisions become as popular as many had hoped.

Organisations are becoming increasingly aware of the impact their perceived environmental credentials have on their reputation, whether that be through their corporate social responsibility initiatives, their position in environmental performance tables, or from the duties placed on directors to consider and report on their company's environmental performance.

Landlords and developers keen to fill voids in an uncertain market are reluctant to do anything that makes agreement of a lease or the sale of a property less attractive. It means that parties are less inclined to move away from the standard lease precedent. Especially now in tough economic times, neither landlords or tenants wish to spend additional money on alterations to bring premises up to an enhanced standard of environmental performance.

Parties also do not want to bear any extra cost associated with negotiating provisions that appear unusual and begin to make the deal less commercially attractive.

There are several measures of assessing the environmental performance of a building, such as BREEAM which sets the standard for best practice in sustainable building design, construction and operation and LEED otherwise known as Leadership in Energy and Environmental Design. What has proved harder to measure is the impact of improving the environmental performance of a building on its value.

Until there is clear data proving that environmental initiatives and performance have a positive impact on value (or that not to implement such initiatives would have a detrimental effect on value), there is no apparent financial incentives for a landlord or developer to spend money on environmental enhancements.

There is little widespread evidence that funders are requiring green lease provisions to be incorporated in to a lease (other than a review of the energy performance certificate) or green leases to be in place as a condition of funding. Whether this changes as lenders try to improve their image in the marketplace is hard to predict. Given the current difficulties in securing finance for property transactions, it is probable that further conditions will be widely resisted, despite a borrower's enthusiasm for environmental initiatives.

There is no doubt a need to improve sustainability given the world's dwindling natural resources and so I predict the green lease will feature more in the marketplace, especially with a renewed effort by the Government to provide incentives for environmental improvements.

Chapters 7

Time to take action!

Hopefully, by the time you have got to this chapter you have found the book to be engaging and informative. To ensure that you stay focused and get the most out of it, please read on and reflect on the previous chapters. The book intends to illustrate how the impact of entrepreneurship has developed over the years pinpointing key examples in history from which we can learn. Learn from the best and consider how the business environment is changing to ensure that you take the right steps and successfully ride the next wave of change that we are encountering. The greats in Chapter 2 would not have been able to achieve their success without partnering with the right individuals. Steve Jobs found Wozniak, Watt found Boulton, Kroc found Sonnberg etc. It's all about creating the right partnerships at all levels to ensure that people are most creative! This stems from the premiss that we all have strengths/talents and weaknesses. It is important to build a winning partnership where each partner brings different complementing strengths to form a productive, magical synergistic relationship!

Whilst the entrepreneur needs to be able to make quick decisions, there are times when they should reflect, consult and consider before taking important steps and decisions. Adopt a winning mindset and eliminate bad habits. "We are what we repeatedly do. Excellence, then, is not an act, but a habit." Aristotle.

To ensure that you cut the risks of failure, take account of the eight points in chapter 4 and seek the right expert advice. At Business 2012 at the O2, I recall Richard Branson saying that had he gone to an accountant for advice before be launched Virgin Records he probably would have been advised against the venture. I believe the point he was trying to make was do not let anybody say you cannot do it. He is absolutely right; so, all the more important that the experts you pick appreciate the entrepreneurial mindset to help you realise your dream rather than dampen your spirits. Where there is a will there is a way.

Chapter 5 illustrates how the entrepreneurial mind if applied is able to acquire property for as little as £1. The great entrepreneur never gives up, as shown in the Chapter 3, and will find a way to achieve his or her target. Today when it is difficult to raise finance, instalment contracts provide an alternative useful creative tool to adopt for the property investor.

Chapter 6 sets out some of the important points to consider when buying an investment property. Property is arguably one of the most valuable and fundamental assets for many of us. It is from this that the entrepreneurs will run their business, live, and invest in.

The Global Entrepreneurship Monitor (GEM) project is a yearly review of the entrepreneurial activity, aspirations and thoughts of people worldwide. It started in 1999 as a collaboration between London Business School and Babson College when the first study covered 10 countries. Now around 100 'National Teams' from every corner of the world have participated in the project, which continues to grow every year. GEM is the largest ongoing study of entrepreneurial dynamics in the world.

GEM explores the role of entrepreneurship in national economic growth, which reveals detailed national features and characteristics connected to entrepreneurial activity. The data collected is analyzed by a central team of experts, which in turn guarantees quality and facilitates cross-national comparisons.

The program has three main objectives:

- To measure differences in the level of entrepreneurship between countries
- To establish what causes the different levels of entrepreneurship
- To suggest policies that may improve the national level of entrepreneurial activity.

GEM is unique because, unlike other entrepreneurship research organizations that measure startups and SMEs, GEM studies, at the grassroots level, the pattern of individuals with respect to starting and managing a business. This method arguably promises a more realistic and detailed picture of entrepreneurial activity than is found in official national statistics.

The entrepreneurial bug appears to be spreading globally. According to the Global Entrepreneurship Monitor Report January 19, 2012, which is the largest of its kind, finds an upsurge in entrepreneurship worldwide. Entrepreneurs are now numbering near 400 million in 54 countries - with millions of new job creation opportunities in the coming years.

The annual survey polled 140,000 adults aged between 18 and 64 from 54 different economies. Following from this GEM estimate 163 million are women early-stage entrepreneurs, 165 million to be young early-stage entrepreneurs (18 to 35 years old), 65 million entrepreneurs plan on creating 20 or more jobs in the next five years, and 69 million offer innovative products or services that are new to the market.

According to Donna Kelley, Babson College professor and the study's author, "Even better news is that over 140 million of these entrepreneurs expect to add at least five new jobs over the next five years. These figures and growth projections affirm that entrepreneurial activity is flourishing across the globe and that entrepreneurship, as an economic engine, is the best hope for reviving a weakened world economy."

Professor Kelly's findings are very exciting and profound for entrepreneurs and politicians who have the very difficult responsibility of improving the economy.

The economy is composed of businesses. Any small business is integral to the economy. Without it, the economy would not survive. However, it is important that the business sustains itself and be able to constantly change to fulfill the needs of the marketplace.

Entrepreneurship produces capital and keeps the

economy afloat, which justifies the importance of innovation in entrepreneurship. Entrepreneurs and businesses see if there is a need within the market and come up with a solution. They grab the opportunity to innovate to make lives more comfortable; and, these solutions keep evolving.

Crises have historically spurred great waves of innovation. The world has experienced financial difficulty and uncertainty, which no doubt will lead to a wave of great creativity from the third industrial revolution as described in Chapter 1.

A wide assortment of technologies are advancing at exponential rates and converging. This provides small teams the ability to do what was once only possible for large companies and governments.

The advances in computing and mobile technologies have affected most people in the world. In the short space of 15 years, the Internet has changed the way we shop, work communicate, and think. Knowledge used to be available only to the elite through books such as the *Encyclopedia Britannica*, but is today very easily accessible and free. All of this happened because of the advancement of computers and the introduction of the Internet.

These advances can be found not only in the field of computing but also in areas such as genetics, AI, robotics, and medicine. In the year 2000, for example, scientists at a private company called Celera announced that it had raced ahead of the U.S. government led international effort to decode the DNA of a human being. Using the latest sequencing technology including the data available from the Human Genome Project, Celera scientists developed a working draft of the genome. It took many years and cost billions to reach this milestone.

Today, it is possible to decode your DNA for a few thousand pounds. With the price falling, it is expected that a full genome sequence may cost less than £100 within five years. Genome data will be available for millions, perhaps billions, of people. We will be able to find the correlations between disease and DNA and to prescribe personalized bespoke medications tailored to an individual's DNA. This will lead to a revolution in medicine.

We can now "write" DNA. Advances in "synthetic biology" permit researchers, and even students, to create new organisms and synthetic life forms. Entrepreneurs have created software tools to "design" and "compile" DNA. There are startups that offer DNA synthesis and assembly as a service. DNA "printing" is priced by the number of base pairs to be assembled (the chemical "bits" that make up a gene). Today's cost is about 20p per base pair, and prices are dropping exponentially. Within a few years, it could cost a hundredth of this amount. It has been predicted that like laser printers, DNA printers will be affordable home devices.

DNA is not all we can print! In an emerging field (as seen in Chapter One) called digital manufacturing, 3D printers can produce physical mechanical devices, medical implants, jewellery, and even clothing. These printers use a mouthpiece fixed vertically in an X-Y plotter that releases thin layers of tiny dots of material that build up, layer by layer, to produce a 3D replica of the computer-generated design. It means that they can print the perfect ship in a bottle. The cheapest 3D printers, which print basic objects, currently sell for between £500 and £1000.

It will not be long before we have printers for this price that can print toys and household goods. It is expected that within this decade, we will have 3D printers used in the small-scale production of previously labour intensive crafts and goods. In the next decade, we can expect local manufacture of the majority of goods, 3D printing of electronics, and the rise of a creative class empowered by digital making.

As the new 3-D technology becomes more widespread on site, just-in-time customized manufacturing of products will also reduce logistics costs with the possibility of huge energy savings. The cost of transporting goods should significantly drop in the future because an increasing number of products will be manufactured locally in thousands of micro-manufacturing plants and transported regionally by trucks powered by green electricity and hydrogen generated on site.

Nanotechnology is also rapidly developing. Engineers and scientists are creating many new types of materials such as carbon nanotubes, ceramic-matrix nanocomposites (and their metal-matrix and polymer-matrix equivalents), and new carbon fibres. These new materials enable designers to develop goods that are lighter, stronger and more energy efficient, and more durable than before.

There are major advances happening in Micro-Electro-Mechanical Systems (or MEMS) which is the technology of extremely small devices. It is becoming possible to build less expensive gyroscopes used in cars to detect yaw, equally accelerometers in cars, and temperature, pressure, chemical, and DNA sensors. In the future iPhone type cases will act like medical assistants and diagnose illnesses, smart pills once swallowed will monitor our internals; and tattooed body sensors that monitor heart, brain, and body activity.

The new digital manufacturing process will save vast amounts of energy and costs, from reduction in materials used to less energy expended in making products. This should result in an increase in energy efficiency beyond anything imaginable in the First and Second Industrial Revolutions. When the energy used to power the production process is renewable and generated on site, the full impact of this Third Industrial Revolution becomes strikingly apparent.

In short we are innovating at an unprecedented rate. In this and the next decade, we will begin to make energy abundant, inexpensively purify and sanitize water from any source, cure disease, and see an increase in SMEs competing more effectively with the larger organizations. The best part to note is that it will not be the governments that will lead this change it will be the world's entrepreneurs.

Share your thoughts with me once you have read this book. Join me in encouraging ethical effective entrepreneurship and let us ride this innovative wave together!

All the best
The Entrepreneurial Property Lawyer™

P.S.Who is your greatest entrepreneur of all time?

Chapter 8

Useful Information and Links

This section is aimed as an aide memoire which you can refer to during the book or afterwards. It has bite size morsels of information; food for the entrepreneurial mind to help it buzz as I like to say!

"Austerity"

In economics, austerity refers to a policy of deficit-cutting achieved by decreasing spending by reducing the amount of benefits and public services provided. Such policies are used by governments to try to reduce their deficit spending and are usually undertaken with increases in taxes.

Those who advocate austerity reason that a major reduction in government spending can change future expectations about taxes and government spending, encouraging private consumption and result in overall economic expansion.

However, critics do argue that, in periods of recession and high unemployment, austerity policies are counter-productive, because: a) reduced government spending can increase unemployment, which leads to an increase in "safety net" spending while reducing tax revenue; b) reduced government spending reduces GDP, which means the debt to GDP ratio examined by credit rating agencies does not improve; and, c) short-term government spending financed by deficits supports economic growth when consumers and businesses are unwilling or unable to spend or do business.

"Blog"

This is an online two way channel which allows the blog owner/creator to share specialized content with existing and prospective clients and customers and to engage with them.

"BIS"

The Department for Business, Innovation and Skills (BIS) is the government department that supports sustained growth and higher skills across the economy.

The Government of the day has the responsibility to create the conditions for the private sector to grow and remove unnecessary barriers that can stifle growth. It is the role of BIS, as the Department for Growth, to help facilitate this by investing in skills, removing unnecessary regulation, strengthening trade between countries, boosting innovation and helping people start and grow their own businesses.

Visit www.bis.gov.uk

"British Property Federation"

The British Property Federation is a membership organisation focused at representing the interests of all those involved in property ownership and investment.

It concentrates on creating the conditions in which the property industry can develop and thrive, for the benefit of its members and of the economy as a whole.

As its membership includes the biggest companies in the property sector from property developers, owners, fund managers, investment banks and professional organisations that support the industry the BPF is able to provide key insight and expertise needed by legislators (the UK and Scottish governments) and regulators (including various financial, planning and environmental bodies). This valuable feedback is aimed at improving the industry.

Visit www.bpf.org.uk/en/index.php

"Companies House"

The United Kingdom has enjoyed a system of company registration since 1844. Today, company registration is dealt with in law, by the Companies Act 2006.

All limited companies in England, Wales, Northern Ireland and Scotland are registered at Companies House, an Executive Agency of BIS. There are over 2.7 million limited companies registered in the UK, and over 400,000 new companies incorporated each year.

Its main functions are to:

* incorporate and dissolve limited companies;
* examine and store company information provided

under the Companies Act and related legislation; and

- provide this information to the public.

"Collective Leasehold Enfranchisement"

The term given to the statutory right that a leaseholder has either to purchase a lease extension or to collectively purchase the freehold together with the other leaseholders in the building.

"Creative Destruction"

Sometimes known as Schumpeter's gale, is an economic term which has since the 1950s become most frequently linked with the Austrian American economist Joseph Schumpeter, who modified it from the work of Karl Marx and popularized it as a theory of economic innovation.

"Creative destruction" describes the method in which capitalist economic development stems from the destruction of some previous economic order, which is mainly the thrust implied by Werner Sombart, who has been credited with the first use of these terms in his work *Krieg und Kapitalismus* ("War and Capitalism", 1913). In the earlier work of Marx, however, the idea of creative destruction implies not only that capitalism destroys and reconfigures previous economic orders, but also that it must continually devalue existing wealth (whether through recession, dereliction, or war) in order to clear the ground for the creation of new wealth.

In Capitalism, Socialism and Democracy (1942), Joseph Schumpeter developed the concept out of Marx's views (to which the whole of Part I of the book is devoted), arguing (in Part II) that the creative-destructive forces released by capitalism would eventually lead to its downfall as a system.

"David Ogilvy CBE 23 June 1911-21 July 1999"

David Mackenzie Ogilvy, CBE, was an advertising executive and often called "The Father of Advertising." At the age of 38 he wanted to enter the world of advertising with no real experience. A London agency hires him and three years later he became the most famous copywriter in the world building a very well recognised global business. The Ogilvy group was eventually taken over by WPP and is now the world's largest marketing communications firm.

"I doubt whether any copywriter has ever had so many winners in such a short period of time," he wrote in his autobiography. "They made Ogilvy & Mather so hot that getting clients was like shooting fish in a barrel."

"Confessions of an Advertising Man" was his best seller which has become one of the most popular and famous books on advertising.

"Destructive innovation"

Disruptive innovation, a term created by Clayton Christensen, describes the process where a product or service initially starts in simple applications at the bottom of a market and then relentlessly moves up market, eventually displacing established competitors. Examples include telegraphy and telephones, concorde and private jets

If companies tend to innovate faster than their customers' needs, they eventually end up producing products or services that are actually too sophisticated, too expensive, and too complicated for many of the customers in their market.

Companies pursue these "sustaining innovations" at the higher tiers of their markets since this is what has historically helped them succeed; by charging the highest prices to their most demanding and sophisticated customers at the top of the market, companies will achieve the greatest profitability.

However, by doing so, companies unwittingly open the door to "disruptive innovations" at the bottom of the market. An innovation that is disruptive permits an entire new collection of consumers at the bottom of a market access to a product or service that was historically only accessible to consumers with a lot of money or a lot of skill.

Characteristics of disruptive businesses, at least in their early stages, can include lower gross margins, smaller target markets, and simpler products and services that may not appear as attractive as existing products or services from a commercial performance point of view. As these lower tiers of the market offer lower gross margins, they are unattractive to other firms, which aspire to move upward in the market, creating space at the bottom for new disruptive competitors to emerge.

"The Department for Communities and Local Government"

The Department for Communities and Local Government is a ministerial department that works to move decision-making power from central government to local councils so to:

- decentralize power as far as possible
- help people's housing aspirations
- put communities in charge of planning
- increase accountability
- let people see how their money is being spent.

The Department sets policy on supporting local government, communities and neighbourhoods, regeneration, planning, housing, building, fire and the environment. The Department wants to move away from top-down government by giving new powers to communities and the council.

Visit www.communities.gov.uk

"Entrepreneurship"

The capacity and willingness to develop, organize and manage a business venture together with its associated risks in order to make a profit. The most common example of entrepreneurship is the starting of new businesses. Entrepreneurial spirit is characterized by innovation and risk-taking, and is an integral part of a nation's ability to succeed in an ever changing and increasingly competitive global market.

"Freeholder"

When you are the absolute owner of the property. As owner, you are not obliged to pay rent or service charges to anybody, as you would do if you were a leaseholder. The freeholder of a property can grant a lease or tenancy for a rent to another party known as the tenant or leaseholder. The lease or tenancy agreement will set out the arrangement between the parties, namely the period of the agreement, the rent and service charge, the extent of the property, repairing obligations, and rights over the property.

"Free-market capitalism"

An economic system where prices for goods and services are set freely by the forces of supply and demand and are allowed to reach their point of equilibrium without intervention by government policy. This supports highly competitive markets, private ownership and productive businesses. Capitalism grew during the industrial revolution, as described in Chapter 1, being a period of history when innovation and entrepreneurship began to flourish.

According to some historians, the modern capitalist system was created from the conflict between land owning aristocracy and the agricultural producers known as the serfs. Serfs were forced to produce for landlords, who had no interest in technological innovation as they produced to sustain their own families. As landowners did not produce to sell on the market, there was no competitive pressure for them to innovate. The great famine in 1315-1317 and Black Death in 1348-1350 led to decline in agricultural production, which eventually gave rise to capitalism.

"Global Entrepreneurship Week"
12-18 November 2012

"It is about growing enterprise ambition and ensuring that those with ideas know where to get the support they need to make them a reality. It's about creating jobs and opportunities: small business in

the UK employs nearly 60 per cent of the workforce
and contributes almost half of UK turnover."
David Cameron, Prime Minister

Global Entrepreneurship Week – which began life
in the UK back in 2004 as Enterprise Week – is the
world's largest campaign to promote entrepreneurship,
and is recognised by organisations all over the UK as the
highlight of the entrepreneurship calendar.

"The Great Depression"

The Great Depression of 1929-33 was the most severe
economic crisis of modern times. Millions of people lost
their livelihood, and many farmers and businesses became
insolvent. Industrialized nations and those supplying
primary products (food and raw materials) were all
affected in one way or another.

Though the U.S. economy had gone into depression
six months earlier, the Great Depression arguably began
with a catastrophic collapse of stock-market prices on the
New York Stock Exchange in October 1929. In the course
of the next three years, stock prices in the United States
carried on falling and by late 1932 they had dropped to
only about 20 percent of their value in 1929. Despite
ruining many thousands of individual investors, this rapid
decline in the value of assets greatly put pressure banks
and other financial institutions, especially those holding
shares in their portfolios. Consequently, many banks were
forced into financial difficulty; by 1933, 11,000 of the
United States' 25,000 banks had failed. The closure of so
many banks, coupled with a general and nationwide loss
of confidence in the economy, led to vast reduced levels of
spending and demand and therefore production too, which

had a negative domino effect. The result was drastically falling output and drastically rising unemployment.

The Great Depression began in the United States, but swiftly became a worldwide economic problem owing to the close relationships that had been forged between the United States and European economies after World War I. The United States ended the war as the major creditor and financier of post war Europe, whose national economies had been greatly weakened by the war itself and by by war debts. Once the American economy slumped and the flow of American investment credits to Europe dried up there was an automatic negative knock on effect. The Depression hit hardest those nations that were most deeply indebted to the United States, which included Germany and Great Britain.

Almost all countries sought to protect their domestic production by introducing tariffs, raising existing ones, and setting quotas on foreign imports. The effect of these steps was to greatly reduce the volume of international trade and by 1932 the total value of world trade had reduced by more than half as country after country took measures against the importation of foreign goods.

The Great Depression had important consequences in the political arena. In the United States, economic misfortune led to the election of the Franklin D. Roosevelt Democrat as president in 1932. Roosevelt introduced a number of major changes using increased government regulation and massive public works projects to promote recovery. However, despite active intervention, mass unemployment and economic stagnation remained, even though it was on a reduced scale, with approximately 15 percent of the work force still unemployed in 1939 at the outbreak of World War II. The depression ended completely soon after the United States' entry into World War II in 1941 as American factories were flooded with orders from overseas for ammunitions.

"HM Land Registry"

Is the government department formed in 1862 to register the ownership of land and property in England and Wales.

It holds and maintains the Land Register, where more than 23 million titles are documented, as evidence of ownership.

Once land or property is entered in the register, any later ownership changes that affect the title such as a new mortgage or lease are noted as evidence. Anyone who suffers loss because of an error or omission in the register, will usually be compensated.

The Land Registry is part of BIS.
Visit http://www.landregistry.gov.uk/

"Marriage Value"

The additional value to the leaseholder that arises from the "marriage" of the leasehold and the freehold interests once the flat owner has acquired the freehold interest.

The sum of the values of each separate interest is less than the value of the single merged interest and that difference is called "marriage value".

There is no marriage value payable on properties with more than 80 years left to run. This is why it is important to consider extending your lease with around 89 years to run. The longer you leave it the more expensive it becomes especially when it drops below 80 years.

"NHBC"

NHBC (National House-Building Council) is the leading warranty and insurance provider and standards setter for UK house building for new and newly converted properties. As a non-profit distributing company, it reinvests its income in achieving its primary goal; improving quality in house building to protect the homeowner. Make sure your new home developer has this guarantee or equivalent.

NHBC celebrated its 75th anniversary in 2011.

"Intellectual Property Office"

Is the official government body responsible for Intellectual Property (IP) rights in the United Kingdom which include:

- Patents
- Designs
- Trade marks
- Copyright

It is an Executive Agency of BIS. It advocates innovation by offering an accessible and widely understood IP system.

"Jeremy Rifkin"

"The president of the Foundation on Economic Trends and author of 17 best selling books on the impact of scientific and technological changes on the economy, the workforce, society and the environment. His books have been translated in to more than thirty languages and are used in thousands of universities, corporations and government agencies around the world" TED

The five pillars of Mr Rifkin's Third Industrial Revolution are:

1. **Shifting to Renewable Energy:** Renewable energy in the forms of, wind, solar, hydro, geothermal, ocean waves, and biomass. Even though these energies still account for a small percentage of the global energy mix, they are developing quickly as governments seek targets for their widespread introduction into the market and their falling costs make them increasingly competitive.

2. **Buildings as Power Plants:** New technological discoveries now make it possible to design and build properties that create all of their own energy from locally available renewable energy sources, permitting us to see the future of buildings as "power plants". The commercial and economic implications are great and far reaching for the property industry globally. 25 years from now, it is predicted that, millions of homes, offices, industrial and technology parks will be built to serve as both "power plants" and places to live and work. These buildings will collect and generate energy locally from the sun, wind, agricultural, garbage and forestry waste, ocean waves enough energy to provide for their own power needs including surplus energy that can be shared.

3. **Deploying Hydrogen and Other Storage**

Technologies: Such facilities to be built in every building and throughout the infrastructure to store intermittent energies. To maximize renewable energy and to minimize cost it will be essential to create new storage methods that facilitate the conversion of intermittent supplies of these energy sources into reliable assets. The storage medium that is widely available and can be relatively efficient is hydrogen. It is the universal medium that "stores" all forms of renewable energy to assure that a stable and reliable supply is available to generate power which will also be important for transport.

4. **Using Internet Technology to Transform the Power Grid:** World-wide power grids will be transformed into an energy sharing inter-grid that acts similar to the Internet. To be able to use of the world's power grid akin to the lines of the internet, will allow businesses and homeowners to produce their own energy and share it with each other. The new smart grids or inter-grids will revolutionize the way electricity is produced and delivered. Millions of existing and new buildings will be converted or built to serve as "positive power plants" that can capture local renewable energy e.g. solar, wind. These energy sources will be used to create electricity to power the buildings, while sharing the surplus power with others across the inter-grids, as we now produce our own information and share it with each other across the Internet.

5. **Transitioning the Transport Fleet to Electric,**

Plug-in and Fuel Cell Vehicles: Transport fleet vehicles will be modified to a form that can buy and sell electricity on a "smart continental interactive power grid." The electricity produced in the buildings from renewable energy will also be used to power electric plug-in cars or to create hydrogen to power fuel cell vehicles. The electric plug in vehicles, will also serve as portable power plants that will sell electricity back to the main grid.

"Joseph A Schumpeter 8 February 1883 – 8 January 1950"

The growing attention to entrepreneurs as agents of historical change in the economy was supported by the theoretical work of Mr J Schumpeter. His ideas helped establish entrepreneurship as a substantive area of historical research and strengthened the importance of business historians' efforts by linking entrepreneurship to a theory of economic change. He argued that the essence of entrepreneurial activity lay in the creation of "new combination" that disrupted the competitive equilibrium of existing markets, products, processes and organizations (Schumpeter 1947).

The research of entrepreneurship owes much to his contributions. He is arguably the first scholar to develop theories in this field. His main theories are often referred to as Mark I and Mark II. In the first one, Schumpeter argued that the innovation and technological change of a nation come from the entrepreneurs, or wild spirits. Mark II was developed when Schumpeter was a professor at Harvard. He professed that the agents that drive innovation and the economy are the larger companies, which have the resources and capital to invest in research and development.

On 17 September 2009, The Economist inaugurated a column on business and management named "Schumpeter". The publication has the history of naming columns after significant figures or symbols. The initial Schumpeter column praised him as a "champion of innovation and entrepreneurship" whose writing showed an understanding of the benefits and dangers of business that proved far ahead of its time (Schumpeter 17 September 2009 "Taking fight" Economist.com).

From Capitalism, Socialism and Democracy-one of his most popular books

"The fundamental impulse that sets and keeps the capitalist engine in motion comes from the new markets, the new forms of industrial organization that capitalist enterprise creates."

"This process of Creative Destruction is the essential fact about capitalism. It is what consists in and what every capital concern has got to live in..."

"Nanotechnology"

It is the understanding and control of matter at measurements between approximately 1 and 100 nanometres, where unique phenomena enable novel applications.

A nanometer is one billionth of a metre. A sheet of paper is about 100,000 nanometres thick.

The benefits of this type technology include:

- Certain nanostructures can identify diseased cells and deliver drugs directly to cancerous tumors without harming healthy cells or organs.
- Solar panels incorporating nanotechnology are much more efficient than standard designs in converting sunlight to electricity; promising far more economical solar power in the future.
- Researchers have found how ultra-small specks of rust can aid the removal of arsenic from drinking water.
- For environmental cleanup, researchers have developed a nano fabric that is woven from tiny wires and can absorb 20 times its weight in oil.

Visit http://www.nano.gov/

"Rule of Law"

In essence is a principle that no one is above the law. The phrase roots back to 17th century and was advocated and made more popular in the 19th century by A. V. Dicey. The concept was familiar even to ancient philosophers such as Aristotle, who wrote "Law should govern". The rule of law implies that every citizen is subject to the law. This contrasts with the idea that the ruler is above the law.

The rule of law has been considered as one of the key foundations that determine the credibility and good governance of a nation. The Worldwide Governance Indicators defines the rule of law as: "the extent to which agents have confidence and abide by the rules of society, and in particular the quality of contract enforcement, the police and the courts, as well as the likelihood of crime or violence."

"Social Media"

This is a term, which refers to methods of allowing users to publish content online such as:

- Writing blogs
- Adding comments to others' blogs
- Publishing videos, audio or images on to the Web

Well recognised social media platforms include Facebook, YouTube, Twitter and LinkedIn.

"TED"

Is a nonprofit organisation focused on Ideas Worth Spreading. It formed in 1984 as a conference bringing together people from the worlds of Technology, Entertainment, and Design. Since then it has developed. In addition to the two annual conferences - the TED Conference in Long Beach and Palm Springs every spring, and the TEDGlobal conference in Edinburgh UK each summer, TED hosts the award-winning TEDTalks video site, the Open Translation Project, TED Conversations, TED Fellows, the annual TED Prize and TEDx programs.

It passionately believes in the power of ideas to change attitudes, lives and ultimately, the world. It is building a clearinghouse that offers free knowledge and inspiration from the world's most inspired thinkers and also a community to engage with ideas and each other.

Visit www.ted.com

"SS Business Consultants Limited"

The business consultancy that brings together some of the leading and pioneering consultants from across the world to deliver best practice solutions for SMEs and start ups.

"UK Trade and Investment"

UK Trade & Investment (UKTI) guides UK-based organizations to ensure their success in international markets, and encourage the best overseas companies to look to the UK as their global partner of choice.

Visit www.ukti.gov.uk/home.html

"The World Economic Forum"

This is an independent international organization committed to improving the state of the world by engaging some of the top business, political, intellectuals and other leaders in society to shape such global and regional issues. The annual meeting is held in the Swiss mountain resort of Davos.

References

Chapter 1

Mathias, Peter: The First Industrial Nation: The Economic History of Britain 1700 1914, Routledge, 2001

Rifkin, Jeremy The Third Industrial Revolution www.thethirdindustrialrevolution.com

Chapter2

Carnegie, Andrew: James Watt, librarian, 2009

Israel, Paul: Edison A Life of Invention, 2000

Ford, Henry: My Life and Work, Filiquarian Publishing, 2006

Kroc, Ray: Grinding It Out: The Making of McDonald's, St Martin's Paperback, 1992

Isaacson, Walter: Steve Jobs, Little Brown, 2011

Pritchard, Joseph: Bill Gates: A Biography Kindle Edition, 2012

Janjigian Vaahan: Even Buffet Isn't Perfect, Portfolio, 2009

Branson, Richard Business Stripped Bare, Virgin Books, 2008

Vise A David & Malseed Mark: The Google Story 2005

Chapter 3

Tuchman, Robert: *Young Guns: The Fearless Entrepreneur's Guide to Chasing Your Dreams and Breaking Out on Your Own,* AMACOM, 2009

Covey, Stephen: The 7 Habits of Highly Effective People, Free Press, 2011

Chapter 4

The Companies Act 2006

Haig, Matt: Brand Success How the World's Top 100 Brands Thrive and Survive, Kogan Page, 2011

Rao, Hayagreeva, Sutton, Robert and Webb, P, Allen: Innovation lessons from Pixar: An Interview With Oscar-winning director Brad Bird The McKensey Quarterly April 2008

www.vattenfall.com

Chapter 6

The Department For Business Innovation and Skills website www.bis.gov.uk

The Government's Planning Portal
www.planningportal.gov.uk

Energy Act 2011

BREEAM www.breeam.org

LEED www.leed.net

Chapter 7

The Global Entrepreneurship Monitor website
www.gemconsortium.org

The Third Industrial Revolution Jeremy Rifkin
www.thethirdindustrialrevolution.com

Chapter 8

The Department For Business Innovation and Skills
www.bis.gov.uk

The British Property Federation www.bpf.org.uk

Companies House www.companieshouse.gov.uk

Ogilvy, David: The Unpublished David Ogilvy, Profile,
2012

Christensen, Clayton
www.claytonchristensen.com/ideas-in-action/books/

The Department for Communities and Local
Government www.communities.gov.uk

HM Land Registry www.landregistry.gov.uk

Intellectual Property Office: www.ipo.gov.uk

Jeremy Rifkin The Third Industrial Revolution Jeremy
  Rifkin www.thethirdindustrialrevolution.com

Rothbard, Murray: America's Great Depression;
  CreateSpace 2011

Schumpeter, Joseph: From Capitalism, Socialism and
  Democracy; Routledge; 1994

Nanotechnology www.nano.gov/

TED www.ted.com

SS Business Consultants Limited
  www.ssbusinessconsultants.co.uk

UK Trade and Investment www.ukti.gov.uk/home.html

About the Author

Selchouk Sami LLB (Hons) AIPA is the Founder of SS Business Consultants Limited the business consultancy that brings together some of the leading and pioneering consultants from across the world to deliver best practice solutions for SMEs and start ups. He is also the head of property at a north London firm of solicitors. His experience has been gained from well recognised Legal 500 law firms including a well known insolvency firm. For further information visit www.about.me/Selchouk_Sami